ADVANCE PRAISE FOR

THE LIFE HEROIC
HOW TO UNLEASH YOUR MOST AMAZING SELF

"Elizabeth Svoboda's *The Life Heroic* is the most masterful treatment of heroism available today. Svoboda delves into the heroic potential in each human being, focusing on the latest research and drawing from inspiring real-life tales of heroism. This book is a must-read for both children and adults—it is a true tour-de-force."

—SCOTT T. ALLISON, PSYCHOLOGIST AND AUTHOR OF *HEROIC LEADERSHIP*

"*The Life Heroic* is a step-by-step guide to helping you develop into your most courageous self. What are you waiting for? Become an everyday hero!"

—MICHELLE WERNING, HEROISM EDUCATOR

"Everyone should read and begin to emulate some of the truths in Elizabeth Svoboda's masterpiece. She takes us on a unique journey that will inspire and help train you to become an everyday powerful action hero."

—PHILIP G. ZIMBARDO, PSYCHOLOGIST AND FOUNDER OF THE HEROIC IMAGINATION PROJECT

THE LIFE HEROIC

HOW TO UNLEASH YOUR MOST AMAZING SELF

BY
ELIZABETH SVOBODA

ILLUSTRATED BY
CHRIS HAJNY

Z ZEST BOOKS
MINNEAPOLIS

Zest Books™
An imprint of Lerner Publishing Group, Inc.
241 First Avenue North
Minneapolis, MN 55401 USA

For reading levels and more information, look up this title at www.lernerbooks.com.
Visit us at zestbooks.net.

Main body text set in Caecilia LT Std
Typeface provided by Adobe Systems

Library of Congress Cataloging-in-Publication Data

The Cataloging-in-Publication Data for *The Life Heroic: How to Unleash Your Most Amazing Self* is on file at the Library of Congress.
ISBN 978-1-5415-7860-9 (lib. bdg.)
ISBN 978-1-942186-25-0 (pbk.)
ISBN 978-1-5415-7861-6 (eb pdf)

Manufactured in the United States of America
1-46978-47847-1/4/2019

CONTENTS

INTRODUCTION

It was a cold Tuesday in January 2012, and seventeen-year-old high school senior Graceanne Rumer (now Andreessen) was fighting an afternoon slump after a full day of classes at Philadelphia's Calvary Christian Academy. She hoped to steal a couple minutes of peace and quiet on her bus ride home. "It was a few days before midterms, and I was really worn out," Graceanne says. "I got on the bus and talked to one of my friends—'I'm so tired, I just want to go to sleep.'"

But as soon as the bus got going, thoughts of sleep fled from Graceanne's mind. She watched in horror as the bus driver suddenly went limp at the wheel. He was having a heart attack, and as he slumped over, the bus drifted into an intersection, veering directly into the opposing lane of traffic. Amid the rising panic, one girl said to Graceanne, "You have your license. **Drive the bus!"**

Graceanne knew that at any moment the bus could smash into another vehicle. Though afraid, she sprinted to the front of the bus and took the wheel. She pulled the bus through the opposing lane of traffic in the intersection, and then she guided the vehicle to the side of the road and stopped. Despite the terror and confusion swirling around

WOW

her, she says, something inside just took over. **"I didn't think. I just kind of did it."**

After Graceanne put the bus in park, her heart still hammering, things happened quickly—someone called the police, who soon appeared on the scene. Shaking and disoriented, the young riders got out of the bus and rushed to their relieved families as they arrived. Moms and dads swarmed Graceanne when they learned what she'd done, thanking her for saving their kids. She says, "They were hugging me, like, 'I'm so happy you were there.'"

• •

What would *you* have done in Graceanne Andreessen's situation? Would you have stepped forward and taken the wheel? Before it happened, even Graceanne couldn't have imagined doing something so heroic. Most of us have no idea how we'd respond in a genuine life-or-death emergency, and our impulse might be to think, *That could never be me.*

But it could be you. One day, it might *have* to be you. Self-doubt is understandable, though. Our culture puts heroes on a very high pedestal. In fact, movies today are full of larger-than-life superheroes—Batman, Superman, Wonder Woman, Ms. Marvel, and so on—who fearlessly put themselves on the line to help others. These fictional characters embody a long list of admirable, even superhuman qualities:

selflessness, invulnerability, incredible strength, wisdom. Sometimes, **even real-life heroes can seem superhuman.** Who could possibly match the feats of Martin Luther King Jr., Mahatma Gandhi, Harriet Tubman, and Abraham Lincoln?

In our society, heroes are often presented as almost a different breed of person, as if their accomplishments are beyond what "normal" people could do. But the truth is, the people that we praise as "heroes"— whether they're firefighters, community leaders, or social justice advocates—are everyday human beings, just like Graceanne. They are regular people just trying to succeed at life, and at times they feel confused, vulnerable, and afraid. They second-guess themselves and make mistakes and have days when they wonder whether it's worth it to get up and get dressed. They don't consider themselves superhuman in the least.

Being a real-life hero doesn't mean possessing superhuman strength, having perfect self-control, or never being wrong. Heroism is not some inborn quality that some have more of than others. Anyone can act heroically to help someone in need, and everyone's life is a journey that contains many opportunities to be heroic. Acting heroically is also something we can get better at, just like improving our ability to draw or our jump shot. Psychologist and heroism expert Philip Zimbardo likes to say that most heroes are ordinary. It's the *act* of heroism that's extraordinary.

As you'll see, this book is filled with real stories of ordinary people who acted heroically, and what these stories show is that heroes are defined by their actions, not their abilities. Heroism is about recognizing a need and then acting to help others. Being able to leap a tall building in one big bound is impressive, but it's not heroic unless it's done to save someone. Without that, it's just gymnastics.

The people we praise as heroes feel *connected* to others, and they care about what happens to them. In fact, they care so much that they are willing to put the needs of others first. **Heroes overcome their own wants, desires, doubts, fears, and flaws** in order to make someone else's life better—or sometimes they literally risk their own life to save someone. Graceanne Andreessen was terrified, just like everyone on her bus that January day, but she realized that if she didn't overcome her fear, everyone could be hurt—or worse. Her compassion helped her find the heroic courage to take charge in a dangerous situation.

Graceanne's story highlights another defining quality of heroism: Heroes act when they see a need, not necessarily when it's easiest or most convenient. You know how, when a teacher asks a hard question, everyone shrinks back and glances at one another, hoping someone else will raise a hand? One way or another, heroes resist this impulse. They take action even when it's difficult, risky, and no one else is willing. That might mean speaking out against bullying, feeding someone who's hungry, or grabbing the wheel of an out-of-control bus. We call people heroes when they get off the sidelines even when that's where everyone else is sitting.

Of course, it's important to emphasize that real-life heroism isn't *always* about making split-second, life-or-death decisions. In fact, it rarely is. Most of the time, heroism involves all the less dramatic but still important ways we choose to improve the lives of others. This is what psychologist Philip Zimbardo calls **"everyday heroism"**—and these ordinary selfless deeds, when repeated enough times, can be just as life-changing, or even life-saving. They can also add up to a heroic and satisfying life.

What does this kind of everyday heroism look like? Consider Max Wallack. Max and his great-grandmother, Gertrude Finkelstein, were close as he grew up, but as she got older, she developed Alzheimer's disease, which gradually erodes a person's memory and can change their personality. Eventually, Max's great-grandma could no longer remember basic things, and she became paranoid that her own family members were trying to kill her.

This was very upsetting. Max found it hard to watch how the disease transformed

his once-lucid and loving great-grandma. And after she died, Max wondered if he could find a way to help people and families dealing with Alzheimer's. Then Max learned that working on puzzles can benefit people with memory loss; these activities keep the brain engaged, which may slow the progression of dementia. Even though Max couldn't cure this disease, he got an idea for how he could improve the lives of people dealing with it. So in 2008, when he was twelve years old, Max conceived and founded a nonprofit organization called Puzzles to Remember. He started by donating a handful of jigsaw-style puzzles to the facilities that had assisted his great-grandma.

Max didn't stop there. Even though running a nonprofit required a lot of not-so-glamorous legwork—filling out paperwork, recruiting volunteers, and asking people for donations—Max kept at it, and the nonprofit steadily grew. Today, Puzzles to Remember has donated over ninety thousand puzzles to nursing homes and other care centers across the country, and many have expressed their ongoing appreciation to Max. He says, "I hear back from Alzheimer's caregivers, and they send me photos of patients doing the puzzles."

Acting heroically can be pretty simple, even though it's rarely easy. All it takes is making the choice to help others, and this book will help guide you in how to do that in ways both big and small. What's important is noticing a need and taking action to meet it—even, or especially, when this is hard. Yet the people who do this say that the rewards are more than worth the effort. In fact, research shows that people who help others regularly are **healthier and more fulfilled** than those who only look out for themselves. This is the secret that leads people to become real-life heroes: The more you focus on making things better for those around you, the more full and joyful your own life becomes.

That's a principle Graceanne Andreessen believes in. Saving the other kids on the bus from danger gave her a deep sense of satisfaction that was worth every second of panic and discomfort she went through. "I'm definitely glad that I was able to do it," she says.

With enough heart, preparation, and savvy, you, too, can unleash your most heroic self on the world.

Ready to get started?

1 WHAT IT MEANS TO BE A HERO

Picture the word "HERO" lit up before you, super-sized and blinking like a theater marquee. Now let it slowly fade out. What's the next thing that pops into your head? Is it Superman, flying through the air and stopping trains with his bare hands? Is it Rosa Parks, protesting racial segregation by refusing to leave her seat on an Alabama bus? Or is it someone completely different—someone who may never appear in a comic book or be celebrated with a statue, but who occupies pride of place in your heart?

Whoever you think of most likely represents your heroic ideal. Your own personal heroes represent what heroism means to you, and everyone has their own ideas. In this chapter, we'll consider what it means to be a hero and the main reasons people act heroically. As you'll see, **heroes come in all sizes and descriptions,** and so do heroic actions.

Traditionally, heroes have been defined by selflessness and altruism—so much so that they are willing to risk their own life to save someone else's life (or perhaps a lot of lives) without expecting to get any specific reward. Superman is virtually indestructible, but since his entire life is devoted to using his powers for others, he certainly fits this definition. In real life, people like Harriet Tubman do. Even though she knew she could be caught and killed, she helped hundreds of slaves escape to free territory on the Underground Railroad.

But as Max Wallack's story shows, many other types of selfless acts are also heroic. Heroism doesn't need to be a matter of life and death. Speaking up on behalf of those who are in need or in trouble can be considered heroic, as is the courage to stand up for our most important beliefs. **Selflessness in any form is a heroic quality** even if lives are not at stake. When someone like Max Wallack sacrifices his or her time and works hard to make someone else's life better, that's heroic.

Heroic masters of derring-do—the kind of people who devote their lives to heroism and whose stories make the big screen—are certainly awe-inspiring. But they're not the only ones. If you could somehow gather the world's total heroic population, it would be made up mostly of everyday people who have performed unheralded good deeds. Just ask Ann Medlock, who founded an organization called the Giraffe Heroes Project. Her organization, which started in 1984, celebrates people who "stick their necks out." Of the hundreds of Giraffe Heroes who have been honored over the years, very few have pulled off feats of death-defying bravery. Most are people who work tirelessly to make the world better in their own ways.

In fact, the people we celebrate for their great feats of heroism are often people who *already* practice ordinary acts of kindness all the time. They don't wait for an emergency. They go out of their way to volunteer at schools, to make friends with the new neighbors or the new kid in class, and to make food for people who are sick in bed. Psychologist Philip Zimbardo believes that if we want to live a more heroic life, it's important to develop good habits—routine selfless ways of responding to daily problems. If we practice kindness and everyday heroism consistently, then it feels natural to step forward when a big need comes along or someone is in danger. This is why I suggest that heroes are made and not born. They are often people who make a habit of helping others, so when a serious problem arises, they are trained and ready.

THE MYTHS AND REALITY OF HEROISM

People have all kinds of opinions about what being a hero means. Some of these ideas are fantasies. They come from comic books, myths, and popular culture, and they don't match what real-life heroes actually do. To help separate myth from reality, I've provided two lists below. The first describes the most well-known misconceptions about heroism, and the second describes the ways real heroes behave.

Myths about Heroism

Heroes get all the fame and the glory: True heroes have one primary mission: helping other people. Sure, everyone wants to feel appreciated, and sometimes heroes gain widespread recognition. But that's not why heroes act. Unfortunately, **most everyday heroes don't make the news** or lead parades. "The hero's journey is *not* becoming rich and famous and fabulously successful," says Scott Allison, coauthor of *Heroes: What They Do and Why We Need Them.* "True heroes do the right thing even when no one's looking."

Heroes act alone: Big-screen superheroes are often shown saving the day all by themselves. That's malarkey, and it's one reason being a hero can seem so intimidating. In real life, being a successful and effective hero often means knowing when and how to get help from others (which I discuss in chapters 4 and 9).

Heroes are willing to risk everything: Real heroes have to be ready to sacrifice their lives at any moment, right? No, not at all. In fact, the whole point, even in deadly situations, is for everyone to remain alive. Obviously, that's the only way heroes can continue helping others and doing good. Then again, acts of heroism often involve some type of risk or sacrifice: Heroes help others even when it takes time and costs money, or even when others disagree or oppose them.

THINK

Smart heroes try to minimize risks and protect themselves, even if they can't eliminate danger. This kind of shrewd risk-taking requires **"situational awareness,"** which is a skill you can learn (and which I describe in chapter 7).

Heroes always rescue the weak: Heroes provide help, but that doesn't mean that the people being helped are weak. At some point, all people need help, and all people are capable of giving help and becoming heroes. The person who's being saved one day might save someone else the next. Real heroes want to help everyone fulfill and realize their own heroic potential.

Heroes wear flashy costumes and have special powers: Well, heroes can dress up--a group of people calling themselves Real Life Super Heroes get a kick out of wearing masks and Spandex as they do helpful things, like donating clean clothes to the homeless. But in real life, heroes don't usually wear costumes or need special powers. All that's required is the willingness to put your (nonsuperhuman) abilities to use.

The Reality of Heroism

Real heroes fight, but only when necessary: Even military and police heroes—who are revered for putting their lives on the line to protect others and to defend causes and communities—fight only as a last resort. **Real heroes try to solve conflicts** in ways that protect everyone.

Real heroes heal and take care of others: Many real heroes try not to fight at all. Instead, they use their compassion and skills to heal and save lives. These heroes often belong to the "helping professions"—such as doctors, nurses, EMTs, psychiatrists, and counselors—who make serving others their job.

Real heroes care about social injustice: Some heroes devote their lives to ending injustice, oppression, and discrimination. They seek a fairer and more just society for all. One example is Mahatma Gandhi, whose 1930s Salt March—a protest against British officials who refused to let Indians make salt from seawater—shined a spotlight on India's growing independence movement.

Real heroes bring people together: Political and community leaders become heroes when they use their positions of power to improve people's lives as much as they can. Prime examples include British prime minister Winston Churchill, who rallied his embattled nation to defeat Nazi Germany, and Golda Meir, the Israeli leader who devoted herself to promoting peace in the Middle East.

Real heroes are kind to everyone: Real heroes consistently help others, even when the only recognition they will get comes from the person being helped. They bring meals to people who are sick, for instance, or care for their elderly neighbors. These acts won't be broadcast on CNN, but they are a **key part of every strong community.**

Real heroes use their voices, not just their muscles: Real heroes don't seek fame, but they aren't silent. They're willing to put their reputations at risk to speak out for what's right, even when others might fear or hate them. One example is Bennet Omalu, a Nigerian-American doctor who spoke the truth about how playing football can cause brain damage even when the National Football League attacked him.

Real heroes do their homework: It's true—some heroes spend the better part of each day standing behind lab benches, making discoveries that transform people's lives. These scientist heroes include Jonas Salk, who devised the first effective polio vaccine, and Katharine Blodgett, who figured out how to de-ice airplane wings to make flying safer.

Real heroes devote their lives to others: Real heroism isn't about "sacrificing" your life for others, but it does mean pledging to help others. However, in the mold of Mother Teresa of Calcutta, some heroes devote their entire lives to heroic efforts. Exhibit A: Christoph von Toggenburg, who rode his bicycle thousands of miles across Europe and Asia to raise money for leprosy sufferers.

Real heroes inspire and empower others to be heroes: Some heroes are blessed with strong speaking and writing talents, and they are particularly good at spotlighting injustices or teaching people how to tap their own heroic potential. In one way or another, many heroes try to help others become heroes themselves.

WHY BE A HERO?

As the lists above make clear, leading a heroic life is about what you do, day by day, to help others. This is why **being a hero is within reach** of anyone, old or young, rich or broke, athletic or clumsy.

But why try to be a hero in the first place? It's an important question to ask. A heroic life—no matter what form it takes—is not for the faint of heart. In pursuit of their world-bettering goals, heroes may have to sacrifice all kinds of things: time hanging out with friends, getting perfect grades, saving for a car or a home, and hours of sleep. They might find themselves locked in conflict with people who don't like what they're up to. In extreme situations, they might even have to put their own comfort or well-being at risk.

Given all that, it's only natural to consider: What is it about the heroic life that justifies the sacrifices and effort?

The short answer is that **helping others can be highly satisfying** in ways that almost nothing else can match. There's nothing wrong with wanting a good, comfortable life. Even heroes want to be successful and admired. Who doesn't? Our culture certainly seems obsessed with success and popularity, and social media only amplifies our natural urge to impress others. Even when we know it's superficial, we can easily to start to measure our self-worth by our Twitter followers, our relative hotness, and the number of likes we amass on Instagram. When these go up, we tend to feel happy and pleased: The more people admire us, the more we seem to *matter*, and the happier we feel.

But as you may have noticed, this type of happiness doesn't last. Inevitably, someone comes along who has more followers, looks more attractive, and has more money and success, and we become depressed. Sometimes life breaks our way, and sometimes it doesn't. If we're too dependent on other people's approval, our emotions can become a roller coaster of ups and downs.

Strangely enough, in the long run, research has found that how rich, famous, or attractive we are has almost nothing to do with how happy we feel. Studies of lottery winners have found that people who become insanely rich overnight don't become much happier than they were before. And sometimes, they actually feel a lot worse.

The Lasting Satisfaction of Helping Others

If becoming an instant millionaire doesn't lead to lasting happiness, what *does?*

As it turns out, acts of everyday heroism. In study after study, the results are clear: The happiest and healthiest people are those who connect with others and work to improve their lives. People who help others or serve their community experience a **"helper's high."** They feel happier and more energized, according to Fordham University's Allan Luks. Not only that, but helping others builds strong relationships, which is what tends to make people the happiest over the long term.

One reason helping others can boost our well-being is that it shifts our brain's focus dramatically. When we focus on others—or on big goals that help many people, and not just ourselves—we tend to focus more on accomplishing that goal than on our own flaws and what others think of us. In short, the more hours we spend being selfless, the fewer hours there are to be self-centered. Plus, **making a difference in the world** satisfies our hunger for true purpose in life—a hunger that social media can't satisfy.

Consider your own past experiences to see if this is true for you. Think of a time when you helped others—anything from reading to younger kids at your school to grocery shopping for your grandparents. How did you feel, both while you were helping and afterward? Even if you had to talk yourself into helping at first, do you look back on the experience and feel like it was worth the time and effort? Does knowing that you helped give you a sense of pride?

From here on, make it a point to keep this helping-and-happiness principle in mind, and evaluate it for yourself. "Keep track of how it feels good to help other people," psychologist Robin Rosenberg suggests. Real-life heroes often discover early in life that helping others not only creates lasting satisfaction, but it gives them a rush. That feeling makes them want to help again and again, and over time, generosity becomes part of who they are.

In chapter 9, I tell the story of TJ Berry, who has raised money with his friends to fight hunger, and TJ says, "It makes you feel really, really good when you calculate out how many people you're helping."

Another example is Marcos Ugarte. In September 2012, Marcos—then a high school freshman in Troutdale, Oregon—saw flames rising from his neighbor's house.

He also saw his neighbor's eight-year-old son, Cody Ma, trapped in an upstairs room.

Marcos didn't waste time. He grabbed a ladder, climbed up to the second-story window, punched through the screen, and carried Cody down to safety. "It was just knowing that I had to do the right thing," Marcos says modestly. "Anyone could have done it."

That may be true, but in that moment, Marcos was the one who had the opportunity. And even though he was amped up and in danger the whole time, he did it. Afterward, Marcos felt a sense of joy that you just can't get from, say, buying a new outfit or having a marathon PlayStation session. And Marcos will probably always feel good about himself for helping someone in trouble.

The Greek philosopher Aristotle called this kind of lasting happiness *eudaimonia*—and he called short-lived, ephemeral happiness *hedonia*. Eudaimonia is much more profound than the momentary pleasures of hedonia, such as eating an ice cream cone or pranking your best friend. Eudaimonia is the lasting satisfaction you get from knowing that you've **lived up to your highest potential.** "As it is not one swallow or one fine day that makes a spring," Aristotle wrote, "so it is not one day or a short time that makes a man blessed and happy."

Having a great time at an amusement park is happiness that lasts a day. Heroic actions that help others provide this, too—since many people feel a "helper's high" in the moment—but they also provide a lasting sense of satisfaction and fulfillment.

If you want to taste eudaimonia for yourself, it's easy. Just look around, find someone who needs help, and be the one to help them.

PROFILES IN COURAGE
Chesley Sullenberger

As January 15, 2009, dawned, US Airways pilot Chesley Sullenberger got ready for what he thought would be an ordinary day's work. He'd been assigned to helm Flight 1549, which was scheduled to travel from New York City's LaGuardia Airport to Charlotte, North Carolina.

Less than two minutes after takeoff, as the plane neared three thousand feet, a giant flock of birds approached. Sullenberger and his copilot, Jeffrey Skiles, heard some sickening thunks, followed by an unusual silence. The fly-by collision had knocked out power to both of the aircraft's engines, and the 123-foot-long plane began falling fast, like a skydiver without a parachute.

This unexpected trial scared Sullenberger out of his mind, but he was able to gather his wits and make some quick decisions. The air traffic controller advised him to land in nearby Teterboro, New Jersey, but the plane was descending so quickly that Sullenberger knew he couldn't reach that

 25

airport. He told the controller, "No, we're gonna be in the river."

Sullenberger knew the Hudson River extended for miles, making it a passable emergency-landing spot. Three flight attendants told people to put down their heads and brace for impact. Less than four minutes after the birds had hit the engines, the plane splashed down into the river, churning up plumes of froth.

Though Sullenberger successfully landed the plane on the water, his work wasn't done. He and the crew helped all 150 passengers out through the cabin's emergency exits. Afterward, Sullenberger made a final trip through the cabin, calling, "Is anyone there?" New York City emergency responders quickly

arrived on the scene, and a fleet of Coast Guard boats motored in to pick up passengers. In the end, every one of the people on board Flight 1549 survived.

Sullenberger's blood pressure was sky-high for weeks after his touch-and-go landing, but he's still proud of the way he was able to step up and handle the situation. "He was phenomenal," passenger Joe Hart told a reporter after the rescue. "The impact wasn't a whole lot more than a rear-end [collision]." Like many real-life heroes, Sullenberger doesn't believe he surpassed the call of duty—**he was simply doing a job he loved** in the best, and safest, way he knew how.

2 FIND WAYS TO HELP

In 2009, Brian King asked his ten-year-old son, Ethan, if he wanted to visit the African country of Mozambique. Brian was used to traveling all over the world—he was a nonprofit executive who worked to repair wells so that residents of developing countries could have access to clean water. Ethan happily agreed to go. The trip sounded like an exciting adventure.

While they were in Mozambique, Ethan and his dad traveled to a series of villages. Brian spent most of his time each day helping to fix the village wells, and Ethan found that, just like at home, he got bored when there wasn't much for him to do. One day, Ethan—a star soccer player at his school—decided he'd brush up on his soccer skills to pass the time. "While my dad and his team were working on their well, I put my soccer ball down and started kicking the ball around," he says.

What happened next was totally unexpected. One village kid ran up to him, then another, and before Ethan knew it, **dozens of kids were swarming around,** wanting to know if they could play, too. "I was like, 'Whoa, where'd all these kids come from?'"

Ethan says. "I guess word gets around pretty fast." Before long, he was able to set up a large-scale game, the ball ricocheting across the earth. It was amazing, Ethan reflected. Through soccer, he'd been able to strike up an instant rapport with these kids.

When it was time to leave the village, Ethan hesitated. Most of the village kids likely lived on less than a dollar a day. They often had to create makeshift soccer balls out of things like trash bags wrapped in twine. "I thought to myself, *I have six or seven soccer balls just sitting in my garage*," Ethan says. So he decided to give the kids his ball as a parting gift. "I said, 'This is yours.' They were star-struck. They couldn't believe I was giving them this real soccer ball."

Later, on the way back home to Michigan, Ethan kept replaying what had happened in his mind—how the kids had reacted in shock, then had gone wild in amazement and delight. Ethan saw that **others had a need that he could help fix,** and he made a decision: He would try to make sure kids living in poverty could have real soccer balls and enjoy the challenge and excitement of playing the game. After talking things over with his family, he decided to start a venture called Charity Ball, with the goal of delivering soccer balls to kids who wouldn't otherwise be able to afford them. Ethan founded Charity Ball as a nonprofit organization in 2010. At first, Charity Ball consisted of just Ethan, his dad, and his mom, Lorie.

THANK YOU

After setting up his organization, Ethan asked local businesses if they'd be willing to donate to his cause. A number said no, but Ethan kept calling in his spare time, and **little by little, he started to see results.** Ethan asked people for money, too, and every twenty-five-dollar donation allowed him to buy a new, high-quality soccer ball to give away. At first, Ethan's dad, Brian, would just pack a few donated balls in his suitcase and give them directly to kids in Mozambique and South Africa. Eventually, as people heard about Ethan's mission, they asked him to speak to large groups. This helped him get the word out and collect even more donations.

Soon, people all over the world were hearing about Charity Ball, and more and more donations poured in. This allowed the organization to place larger soccer ball orders. Today, Charity Ball has distributed more than five thousand balls to kids in more than two dozen countries, including Ethiopia, Zambia, India, and Guatemala.

Ethan is still actively involved in his organization, and he's thrilled when he hears about how the balls are changing kids' lives. One young recipient, Divino Filipe, told *People* magazine in 2014: "Now I own a ball that I can share with my friends and have a team for kids our age."

MAKING CONNECTIONS: THAT AHA MOMENT

Ethan's journey illustrates a number of things about acting heroically. First of all, it's not about standing around waiting for trouble to strike.

"Heroic lives are not just lives where you're standing on a mountaintop ready to jump off and save someone," says Stephen Post, a bioethicist and compassion expert at Stony Brook University. Instead, more often, our connections with people are what lead us to care enough to want to help. Only after Ethan played soccer with kids who didn't have a real soccer ball, and only after he'd experienced the joy of giving them his own ball, did he become inspired to do something.

But what if Ethan had never visited Mozambique, and his father had only told him about the villages that didn't have soccer balls? *Maybe* Ethan would have started Charity Ball, but probably not.

Much of the time, everyday heroism springs from those aha moments that occur when we make a connection with someone who has a problem or a need. Usually, only then do we care enough to sacrifice our own time, effort, and money to help. **Connection comes first, then inspiration.** Plus, only when we genuinely love what we do and who we're doing it for do we tend to stick with difficult or long-term heroic efforts.

If you ever feel like you want to help but aren't sure who to help or how, just pay attention to the people you meet and the things you learn in your own life. Eventually, you will probably experience the kind of aha moment that Ethan did, where you suddenly become **inspired to help people** you care about in a way that is both meaningful and enjoyable.

LEANNE'S BIG HEART

That's what happened with Leanne Joyce. At birth, Leanne was diagnosed with a condition called aortic valve stenosis. This made the valve in her aorta—the body's largest artery—narrower, preventing blood from flowing properly to the rest of her body. Every year, Leanne had to go to the hospital for testing so doctors could check how well her heart and aortic valve were functioning.

One day when Leanne was twelve, she was sitting around at the hospital waiting for her test results to come back, when a group of volunteers walked up. They greeted Leanne and gave her a ten-dollar iTunes gift card. She was grateful someone had thought of her, and the gift helped get her mind off her illness for a while.

About a month later, Leanne got some shattering news. Her doctors told her she had to stop jumping rope, swimming, and doing gymnastics—things she did over twenty hours a week. The doctors said those activities could be dangerous for someone with her condition. "Being told I could no longer do those sports was extremely devastating," Leanne says. "I was really depressed."

Eventually, Leanne came to terms with her physical limits. "I pretty much realized there was nothing I could do to change that situation," she says. Still, without sports, Leanne had a lot of free time on her hands. She thought about the gift she'd gotten at the hospital and how much it had meant to her. In a flash of inspiration, she decided she wanted to use her extra time to raise money to buy gifts for other kids in the hospital.

Leanne's first idea was to hold a bake sale at her local supermarket. But to do that, she had to be registered as an official nonprofit organization. So she started filling out the paperwork to form her own nonprofit. In the meantime, to raise money, she started selling wristbands printed with the name of her organization, Positive Impact for Kids.

After about a year, Positive Impact for Kids finally received its official nonprofit status, and Leanne knew she could **make a difference on a big scale** as word of her mission spread. Through events like tennis fundraisers and 5K charity runs, Leanne has since raised over a hundred thousand dollars—enough money to buy things like gift cards and iPads for young patients at more than a hundred hospitals. "You don't have to start with some huge goal in mind," she says. "I first wanted to just start at a smaller hospital. I never would have imagined donating to 115 hospitals."

Of course, to find ways to help, you don't have to experience an aha moment of inspiration like Leanne's. Simply think about who matters to you and what they struggle with. **What problems in the world stand out to you?** Heroic actions often begin when you notice "something that so upsets your moral compass that you have to do something," says Matt Langdon, founder of the Hero Round Table conference.

The world is an imperfect place, and there are lots of ways you can make it better.

FINDING YOUR HEROIC MISSION

Right now, write down one possible way you might help other people. Keep this idea simple and doable, but identify a problem that matters to you. Make this effort something you truly care about, not something you think you *should* care about. Then keep this heroic mission in mind as you read this book, which will guide you in accomplishing it.

If you need help deciding what a good heroic mission might be, try this quick exercise. It will help you clarify what goals are most meaningful to you and get you started on achieving them.

1. Grab a piece of paper, draw a large square, and draw a tic-tac-toe grid inside of it. You should have nine boxes in total—three rows across and three down.

2. Think about three problems you've noticed in your school, your community, and the world. They can be big problems or small ones—the essential thing is that they're important to you. In the top three boxes of your grid, write down a couple of sentences that describe each problem. You could write things like, "Kids in violent homes can fall behind in school and in life," "Bullying makes kids feel depressed and worthless," or "Some kids with working parents don't have anywhere to go after school."

3. In the second row of boxes in your grid, write down one way you can think of to help solve the problem or to make things better for people who have that problem. What action might you take?

4. In the third row, write down your ideal vision for how this action would help. If you succeeded with your heroic efforts, **what would you hope to achieve for others?**

5. Now, consider the three heroic missions you've written down. All might be great, but which seems the most exciting? Choose that one, and draw a star above that column. You can always change your mind, but start with this one.

TAKING ONE STEP AT A TIME

Once you've identified a problem that fires you up, the next step is putting your desire to help into action. To be honest, this is the hard part, but don't worry: The rest of this book will help you figure out what to do.

Most of all, like Ethan and Leanne, **start out by taking manageable steps.** Just write down one or two specific things you could get done within the next couple of weeks or months. Don't worry about long-term goals right now.

Think about practical ways you could address the problem using your own unique set of strengths. Superheroes harness their special abilities to save the day, and you can do the same thing in real life. Most serious problems are too big for one person to solve, so think about the help you *can* provide. "Think about what *your* power is, or what you want it to be," says psychologist and hero expert Robin Rosenberg. "What are your talents, abilities, skills? What do you want to cultivate, and to what purpose do you want to put it?"

What are some things you could do? You could write an editorial for the school or city newspaper. You could organize a walk-a-thon to raise money for your chosen cause. If acting is your thing, you could write and stage a play about the issue. If you're more into the business side of things, you could raise funds selling popcorn or cotton candy at school events. Or if you like the idea of pursuing your goal with friends, start a school club that addresses the problem.

Often, coming up with a plan and putting it into action isn't very glamorous. That's normal and expected. We don't often think of heroes holding tennis fundraisers, but as Leanne showed, simple everyday actions can be surprisingly effective.

Then, like Ethan and Leanne, ask your parents, teachers, or other adults for input as you brainstorm what to do. Later chapters describe this in more detail, but getting advice and help from others is key. One great way to figure out how to help is to ask people what kind of help *they* need. You may think you know exactly what to do, but others may have ideas you've never thought of. Plus, people appreciate being asked. It shows respect and caring, and all by itself it can help people feel less alone.

At first, what's most important isn't so much what you do as that you do something. Your actions call attention to the problem, and once others know about it, they may join in to help, too. Many people *think about* making positive change, but a surprisingly small number actually turn those lofty intentions into action. If you do that much, you'll be on your way to a heroic life.

Finally, don't put too much pressure on yourself to achieve a particular result. Just **make your action plan,** start working on it, and see how things unfold. At the beginning, "it doesn't have to be this huge thing," Ethan King says. "When I first gave my soccer ball away, I did not imagine at all that I would start an organization." But like Ethan, you may find that **small acts can get big things rolling.** When you stay focused on your heroic goal, the world notices, and your actions may grow in ways you can't predict.

And if you change your mind after a while and decide to choose a different heroic goal, that's okay, too. Don't worry that changing course means your past efforts are wasted—far from it. It's a safe bet that you will learn important lessons while pursuing your heroic goal, and you can put these into practice for your *next* heroic goal. As you'll discover, this is all part of your heroic journey.

HEROES FROM HISTORY
Jan Karski

Can you be a hero even if your best-laid plans get derailed? That's the question Jan Karski's life forces us to consider. A member of Poland's resistance movement during World War II, Karski snuck into the Warsaw ghetto, a disease-ridden holding pen where Jewish people were kept before being sent onward to death camps. Karski's experience convinced him of the terrible truth: The Nazis intended to kill all of Poland's Jews, with no exceptions.

Karski decided he had to alert the American president Franklin D. Roosevelt to what was going on. So he set off on a long, dangerous journey, traveling to Washington, DC, and eventually met with Roosevelt. The American president assured Karski that the Allies would beat the Nazis, but despite Karski's warnings, Roosevelt and the Allied armies did not take specific steps to stop the Holocaust. Karski risked his life to deliver a firsthand report about the horrors unfolding in Poland, but those in power chose not to answer his call to action.

For decades afterward, Karski was upset at this failure. His actions had not stopped the genocide. He second-guessed himself: What could he have done differently? Nevertheless, today, Karski is celebrated as a hero for his committed efforts. Israel's Holocaust remembrance center, Yad Vashem, has recognized Karski as Righteous Among the Nations, the highest honor it bestows upon non-Jewish rescuers.

As Karski's story shows, not every heroic mission is destined to succeed. **But true heroes try anyway.** Sometimes, the best you can do is to accept that you did everything you could, and then make other plans to create positive change.

3 RECOGNIZE YOUR HERO'S JOURNEY

Once you decide to take action to help others, you set out on a journey, whether you realize it or not. To succeed, you'll need to get help from other people and overcome obstacles. You'll probably need to learn new skills and try uncomfortable things. You'll have to take risks, and at times, you'll struggle with doubts, anxiety, and fear. If you persevere, however, not only will you accomplish what you set out to do, but the effort itself will transform you from the inside. By the end, you'll become a smarter, more accomplished, more mature, and more compassionate human being.

In other words, you'll gain many of the heroic qualities we've talked about already.

This **process of personal growth** is often called the "hero's journey," which arose from the work of mythologist and scholar Joseph Campbell. In learning about the myths of cultures from around the world, Campbell recognized that certain stories are repeated almost everywhere. The hero's journey is one of these universal stories, and Campbell described this journey in his book *The Hero with a Thousand Faces.*

The story of the hero's journey symbolizes the process of maturity. It isn't meant to provide instructions for how to be a hero. In this case, *hero* refers to the main character or protagonist of the story. And yet the main character is always trying to accomplish a heroic task: to act selflessly, even altruistically, to help others. That's why the hero's journey provides a good way to think about how to accomplish your own heroic goals. In fact, this book uses the main stages of the hero's journey to help **guide you in pursuing a heroic life.**

You're probably already very familiar with this story. Ever since Campbell first described it, scriptwriters, novelists, and playwrights have used this plot or narrative to craft meaningful movies, books, and plays that stand the test of time.

Have you ever seen *The Wizard of Oz* or *Star Wars?* These tales follow the classic hero's journey formula: a young person yearns for adventure, runs off or gets swept away (say, by a tornado), meets trials and obstacles (flying monkeys, Stormtroopers), gains mentors and helpers (a scarecrow, Obi-Wan Kenobi), learns new skills (how to wield a

lightsaber), and discovers inner resources (the Force, standing up for oneself). After winning the final, ultimate battle against the biggest enemy (the Wicked Witch, Darth Vader), the hero returns home. At the end, the world has been saved and the young person has been transformed into a genuine adult hero because he or she now understands what truly matters (there's no place like home, you must protect those you love).

Does that sound like other classic stories you know? On the surface, these stories might not seem very similar. They could be set on different continents, in different eras, and even in different galaxies. The main characters may not be kids. Some may be kings, queens, or presidents, while others are just regular people trying to get by. But all of the stories follow the hero's journey: The main character faces tough times, battles a series of foes, ultimately triumphs, and emerges transformed.

The reason the hero's journey is a universal myth is because it encapsulates the journey all human beings take in real life. That's why these stories captivate us so much. We see ourselves in the characters as they wrestle with demons and face harrowing obstacles and grow. They bring our own struggles to mind. And when **the characters muster all their ingenuity and grit** to battle the forces that hold them back, they give us hope that we can surmount our own obstacles.

In fact, listening to stories is one way we learn. Recently, scientists at Princeton University discovered that the same areas of the brain light up whether we are telling or listening to a story. This suggests we don't just absorb information when we hear or read a story. We're also living out the story's journey in our minds.

That's why the best, most gripping stories are far more than just entertainment. Seen in the right light, they're also guides for how to handle whatever comes up in life. And once you learn the way stations of the hero's journey, you can mine any story for inspiration as you proceed along *your* heroic path.

STEP BY STEP: THE HERO'S JOURNEY

Joseph Campbell listed **seventeen stages to the hero's journey.** Others have condensed this process down to twelve or eight stages. In this book, I've simplified it even further to six stages. While people like screenwriters and mythologists sometimes use different names for the stages, the basic process or journey I'm describing remains the same.

Here are the six stages I address in this book:

1. The call to adventure
2. The refusal of the call
3. Seeking mentors and allies
4. Overcoming tests and obstacles
5. The final ordeal
6. The return

1. The Call to Adventure

The first stage of the hero's journey is usually a call to adventure. The main character is chugging along, living life as usual, when something happens that completely changes the world as he or she knows it. Picture Luke Skywalker in *Star Wars*, spending his days as a farmhand on the planet Tatooine. Then he meets a robot that plays a recording of a mysterious woman: "Help me, Obi-Wan Kenobi. You're my only hope."

In this book, we've already discussed the call to heroic action in chapter 2. It's that "aha moment" when we realize how we can help someone. It's when Ethan played soccer with village kids in Mozambique and when Leanne realized she could raise money for gifts to cheer up kids in the hospital. **Whenever we hear people ask for help,** or we see people in need, we face a choice, just like Luke does in *Star Wars*: He can try to figure out who the trapped woman is and be the one to help her—or he can just blow the whole thing off.

Except then there'd be no movie.

2. The Refusal of the Call

In fact, the main character in many stories first attempts to ignore the call to adventure. The call might sound interesting, important, and even exciting, but the hero is just not ready to give up the comforts of ordinary life, or he or she fears the challenge or danger. So, in one way or another, the hero refuses the call.

In the Greek epic poem *The Iliad*, the powerful warrior Odysseus is summoned to board a ship to the city-state of Troy to help rescue the Spartan king's captured wife, Helen. But later, afraid of what may happen to him, Odysseus tries to wriggle out of the commitment, even plowing salt into a field so that people will think he's insane.

In real life, people refuse the call to heroic action all the time. Sometimes they refuse the same call for help over and over again. Accepting the call can feel very difficult. In some ways, it's the hero's first test, since you can't start a hero's journey until you accept the call. Another term for committing to act selflessly to help someone is "everyday heroism."

3. Seeking Mentors and Allies

Once the hero accepts the call and starts the journey, he or she must get help. In stories, characters sometimes don't realize they need help until a mentor arrives who offers much-needed encouragement. The mentor might help the hero see him- or herself in a new way, supply an important object the hero will need, or teach skills that the hero can use to reach his or her goal. Think Obi-Wan Kenobi in *Star Wars*, the bearded Jedi master who teaches Luke how to use the Force and how to confront tough situations with courage.

Mentors instill confidence—they urge heroes to

push past their own doubts and fears and convince them that their **goals are within reach.** In stories, heroes tend to meet mentors early on, and at just the right time, inspiring them to commit to the heroic path full tilt. They know their journey won't be easy, but they believe it will be worth the trouble and sacrifice. "There's a transformational moment," says psychologist Robin Rosenberg. "They decide to use [their] talent and power for good."

Stories often feature just one or two mentors, but in real life, we may have many mentors and acquire numerous allies who assist us in our quest to help others. As in stories, these may be people we meet along the way, or they may be people we already know. As I discuss in chapters 4 and 9, these are the people we can reach out to and ask for help and advice.

4. Overcoming Tests and Obstacles

Of course, stories wouldn't be stories without problems. As the hero tries to accomplish his or her goal, the character runs into a slew of obstacles or tests (Campbell called them trials). Typically, at first, nothing goes the way it's supposed to—and often, things only seem to get worse and worse. In *The Wizard of Oz*, Dorothy's trip to the Emerald City is almost derailed several times: by nasty apple trees, by a seemingly dangerous lion (who turns into a friend), and by a field of sleep-inducing poppies. Before Luke

Skywalker battles Darth Vader and the Death Star, Luke's aunt and uncle are killed, Obi-Wan Kenobi is killed, and he has to rescue a captured princess.

As heroes endure these tests, they typically start to doubt themselves and feel discouraged. But they continue to pursue their goals despite their misgivings and fears. And as they confront and vanquish one challenge after another, they learn important lessons that will help them overcome the ultimate or supreme challenge that awaits.

In real life, **obstacles and tests come in all shapes and sizes.** One of the hardest challenges is coping with the doubts of people who don't believe in us and the ridicule of people who don't understand what we're doing. I discuss this further in chapter 5.

5. The Final Ordeal

In stories, the drama builds toward the most critical stage of the hero's journey: the final ordeal, which is typically a confrontation with the main villain or antagonist. This stage presents the biggest test of all—one that forces the hero to come face-to-face with his or her worst fears. Many times, during this battle, heroes know they risk dying or losing everything.

In *Star Wars*, Luke must command an X-Wing spaceship and face heavy enemy fire in order to wipe out the planet-destroying Death Star. In *The Wizard of Oz*, Dorothy and her friends must brave a squad of bloodthirsty flying monkeys to reach the notorious Wicked Witch of the West. After the Witch sets the Scarecrow on fire, Dorothy accidentally douses her with a bucket of water—which turns out to be the ideal strategy. As the Witch melts into a puddle, her former guards exult, "Hail to Dorothy! The Wicked Witch is dead!"

By surviving the toughest challenge, heroes are typically transformed or receive some reward or gift. After defeating the Wicked Witch of the West, Dorothy finally learns how she can return to Kansas and rejoin her family.

6. The Return

In stories, heroic journeys end when the hero returns home. The main character—having passed all the tests, learned the most important lessons, gained allies, and resolved the main problem—is recognized and honored as having matured. Furthermore, the hero typically embraces his or her new role as **someone who will serve and protect the community** from now on. After all, that's what heroes do.

In real life, this relates to what happened with Ethan. His first small heroic act grew into bigger and bigger acts, until it became something that was larger than himself: a nonprofit organization that many people support and work for. Often, we don't know where our heroic actions may lead, and they don't always result in ongoing programs. But, bit by bit, everyday heroic actions do change us—and they can even change the entire trajectory of our lives. This is what I discuss in chapter 10.

MAPPING THE HERO'S JOURNEY

To better understand the hero's journey, you can use this exercise to discover how it's used in your favorite stories. On a piece of paper, draw six columns, and label each column at the top: **the Call to Adventure, the Refusal of the Call, Mentors and Allies, Tests and Obstacles, the Final Ordeal, and the Return.**

Draw a horizontal line underneath the labels, creating a box under each column. Choose a book, movie, or story you love, and consider each of the six stages. Inside each box, write two or three sentences describing how this phase of the journey shows up in the story.

For example, if you've chosen *Harry Potter and the Sorcerer's Stone*, your "Mentors and Allies" box might include a description of Harry's relationship with the half-giant, half-man Rubeus Hagrid, who helps him get through his demanding first year at the Hogwarts School of Witchcraft and Wizardry. For "Tests and Obstacles," you might write about how Harry slips past a fierce three-headed guard dog and, along with his friend Ron, defeats a dangerous troll in the school's dungeon.

Once you've filled out all the boxes, write down some thoughts about how the main stages of the hero's journey apply to experiences in your own life. What challenges have you faced, and **what strategies did you use** to overcome them?

USING THE HERO'S JOURNEY FOR INSPIRATION

How can the classical hero's journey help you pursue your own real-life heroic goals? As you absorb stories—real or fictional—about other people's heroic adventures, you can take heart in the fact that they also encounter big challenges and must muster all their strength to solve them. Reading about these heroes helps you rehearse the feelings and thoughts you'll have as you pursue your own heroic quest.

This chapter's "Profiles in Courage" tells the story of Malala Yousafzai, the Nobel Peace Prize winner who is fighting for girls in Pakistan to get better educations. As we read her story, we *become* her, in a sense. We feel her profound hope that she can create real change by making her voice heard. We also feel her pain, confusion, and anguish, and we take heart when she decides to keep going despite her fear.

In real life, we all want to succeed, and it's frustrating when things don't go our way. We can start to doubt that we're on the right track. Even more, when things don't go as planned, we might be tempted to believe something is wrong with *us*.

But the story of the hero's journey reminds us that life is never easy, especially when our goals are heroic. Life has a way of defying our best-laid plans—and what matters in the journey is **how we respond to setbacks and tests.** If we fail once, will we get the help and learn the skills that will lead to success next time? It's almost as predictable as a math formula: The more audacious our goal, the more likely we are to run into trouble along the way.

By immersing yourself in the heroic journeys of others, you steel yourself for the doubt and frustration you'll face along your own path. Build up a rich mental data bank of heroes, and return to this inner library for solace and inspiration whenever you want. That's why stories like *Star Wars* and Harry Potter are such a crucial part of heroic training. (And you can tell that to your mom when she catches you watching *The Force Awakens* past bedtime.)

USING THE HERO'S JOURNEY STAGES IN REAL LIFE

The stages of the hero's journey never unfold as neatly in real life as they do in stories. In real life, the stages may happen in almost any order. But understanding the stages can help you decide what to do. The mythic sequence of the hero's journey contains a lot of practical advice.

For instance, let's say you notice some new students at your school who have recently arrived from other countries, and they are having a hard time adjusting to school and the United States. So you decide to create a club to help them feel more at home. You remember that heroes need mentors and allies, so you call on your favorite social studies teacher—who's a refugee from Iran herself—to help you plan the club's activities.

Your teacher is thrilled and happy to assist, but your school's administration tells you there's no more money in the budget available for school clubs until next year. But you don't want to wait till next year. These students need help now.

This is frustrating, but you aren't deterred because you know **it's totally normal for heroes to face obstacles.** All you have to do is brainstorm a way to raise the money you need. You start an online call to action and link to it on your Facebook page. Eventually, the money starts to trickle in—five dollars from your best friend, twenty dollars from a next-door neighbor, and a whopping hundred dollars from one of your dad's friends.

After two months, you've raised enough money to run the club, and you pair fifteen new students at your school with peer mentors. You organize several club activities, including a pizza party, a hiking outing, and a trip to a soccer game. Of course, each of these activities involves a new set of obstacles and challenges, and more times than you care to admit, you are tempted to give up. Like Odysseus plowing salt into the field, you sometimes wonder if you should reject the call and walk away.

But you don't. You know that, just like in your favorite stories, **challenges are never going to go away entirely.** In fact, they sometimes only seem to get bigger, but each time you meet them, you are rewarded with inner fortitude and strength. On good days, you feel like you can handle anything that might crop up. You realize, too, that your work isn't done. It's great that the new kids are forging friendships, but you see more people to help and more ways to help them, so you keep going, knowing the rewards—both for you and for others—will make it all worth it.

PROFILES IN COURAGE
Malala Yousafzai

As a child, Malala Yousafzai loved going to school more than almost anything else. Every day, she looked forward to challenging herself and learning things. But the extremist Taliban army occupied her home region in Pakistan—Swat

Valley—in 2007, and in late 2008 Taliban leaders declared that girls in the region would no longer be allowed to go to school. Malala was devastated at the thought of leaving her studies, but her father, Ziauddin, who owned his own school, reassured her he would do everything he could to make sure girls could keep learning. Ziauddin kept his school open even after Taliban militants began bombing girls' schools.

Malala saw her father's brave efforts as a call to action. She joined him in advocating for girls' right to a quality education. She wrote a blog for the British Broadcasting Corporation (BBC) about what life was like in Swat Valley under the Taliban, and later, a *New York Times* journalist made a film about her.

But as Malala's profile rose around the world, Taliban fighters grew more focused on stopping her outspoken mission. She and her father received a variety of death threats, and one attacker almost managed to succeed. As fifteen-year-old Malala was leaving school on October 9, 2012, a bullet from an unknown assassin pierced the air, hitting her in the forehead before lodging in her left shoulder. Afterward, Malala was in critical condition, unconscious and breathing through a ventilator.

Malala survived this massive ordeal with her compassion and determination intact. After she recovered, she continued to promote the education of women and girls, even though she knew she would face more trials and threats. However, thousands of supporters now showered her with praise and chipped in to fund her efforts. "The terrorists thought they would change my aims and stop my ambitions," Malala once said in a speech to the United Nations. "Nothing changed in my life except this: Weakness, fear, and hopelessness died. **Strength, power, and courage was born."**

In the years since then, Malala's caring, integrity, and steely resolve have inspired millions of people all over the world. In 2014, she became the youngest-ever person honored with the Nobel Peace Prize, which is given to those whose work advances harmony between nations. And despite getting caught up in a whirlwind of international fame, Malala remains focused on her original goal: finishing her own education while working to make sure every other girl gets to do the same.

4 SEEK MENTORS AND ROLE MODELS

Think about one person you truly look up to. What do you admire about them? Is it the way they never get flustered in the face of trouble? The way they support you when things go bottom-up? The way they forge ahead and act in ways you can't imagine acting yourself?

In 1999, when Megan Felt was fourteen years old, she wasn't looking for a role model, and she wasn't looking for a way to be a hero. But she got a call to action, anyway. One day, while working on a history project, Megan and her friends read about the little-known story of Irena Sendler, who was a social worker in Poland. During World War II, Sendler heard about the plight of thousands of Jewish children imprisoned in the Warsaw ghetto. With her deep knowledge of Jewish religion, Sendler understood that **both lives and cultural legacies** were in danger, since the Nazis planned to kill the city's entire Jewish population.

Determined to save as many ghetto children and families as she could, Sendler created a network of collaborators to get them out. She improvised many ways to slip people past the guards, like bundling them up in old sacks and smuggling them out in food carts. She gave the escapees false names to hide their identities, writing their real names on slips of paper and hiding them in milk jars that she buried in the ground. **In the end, Sendler rescued thousands of people from near-certain death.**

When Megan first found out about Irena Sendler, she was amazed at her bravery and ingenuity. Questions filled her mind about how the young social worker had managed to carry out her selfless mission. Feeling inspired, Megan and her friends decided to write and produce a play about Irena's life. They called the play *Life in a Jar*.

Life in a Jar was a big hit in the local community, and after a flurry of media coverage, the girls were invited to perform the play hundreds of times all over the country and the world. Eventually, Irena Sendler herself—who was then still living in Poland—heard about the play and began writing to Megan and her friends. They wrote back, and a busy correspondence sprang up. "Before the day you had written *Life in a Jar*, the world did not know our story," Sendler wrote in one of her letters. "Your performance and work is continuing the effort I started over fifty years ago. You are my dearly beloved ones."

As the girls and Sendler wrote back and forth, Megan felt like she was getting to know the older woman on a deeper level. In 2001, Megan crossed the Atlantic to visit her hero in person for the first time, and she could hardly wait to ask the big question that had long been tumbling around in her mind: "Why did you risk your life to save Jewish children?"

At first, Sendler talked about other people who had helped, not herself, but finally she answered: "It was a need of my heart. After the German invasion, Poland was drowning in a sea of tragedy and brutality. And of all the Poles, the Jews were the most in need of aid."

Megan understood. Her Polish friend had known the risks she faced, but she'd gone on with her work because it allowed her to live out her highest values. Understanding the depth of Irena Sendler's commitment to others made Megan **more determined to help people** in trouble, too.

HOW MENTORS AND ROLE MODELS HELP US

Whether we need immediate help with a heroic goal or not, identifying mentors and role models is always a smart move. We should always be on the lookout for people whose lives are examples of the way we would like to conduct our own lives, interact with the world, savor joys, and overcome challenges. Role models show us how ordinary people can lead extraordinary, even heroic, lives.

Having people to admire better prepares us to rebound when life throws challenges our way. In a survey of teenagers who'd been through tough situations, those who had positive role models did better in school and were less likely to get into serious trouble. Role models and mentors can broaden our perspective: Through their example, they help demonstrate how to take a forward-looking approach to life, instead of getting wrapped up in momentary troubles like a botched quiz in biology class. They have a way of reminding us that there's more to life than popularity battles and standardized tests.

 Right now, think about the people you would consider to be role models. Trust your instincts. Most of us are pretty good at sniffing out people who "talk the talk but don't walk the walk"—like the lunch monitor who whisks away your soda while sipping her own fizzy beverage. On the other hand, we're also good at spotting people whose actions *do* match up with their morals—and **these kinds of people impress us profoundly.**

Research has shown that the values and priorities of the people we admire tend to rub off on us. When our role models are people with compassionate, inclusive attitudes, we also become more likely to reach out to others. Certainly, how we view others often determines whether we help them or not.

Malala Yousafzai's most important mentor and role model was her father, Ziauddin. His courage and resolve helped awaken Malala to these qualities in herself. After extremist Taliban forces occupied Malala's home region of Swat Valley, Ziauddin continued to stand up for girls' right to an education even though he knew the Taliban might retaliate. **Ziauddin taught Malala that her ideas and potential mattered** and that she was capable of making a lasting contribution to the world. His heroic actions and mentorship inspired his daughter's heroic actions.

"I encouraged her to sit with me when my friends used to come. I encouraged her to go with me to different meetings," Ziauddin told an audience in Vancouver, Canada, in 2014. "And this was not only she, only Malala. I imparted all these good values to my school, girl students and boy students as well."

Ethan King, who started the Charity Ball organization, has also drawn strength and inspiration from his father. Brian King's work to make sure people around the world have fresh water to drink has influenced both Ethan's work ethic and his concern for others. "I definitely consider my dad a big role model," Ethan says. "He's always challenging me to be a master of my resources, to do everything I can with my time on earth."

A ROLE MODEL RECIPE

Every heroic role model and mentor is unique in his or her own way. But most of them have some basic things in common. As you consider who might help you with your own heroic goals, and what to look for in a role model, keep the following qualities in mind.

They act according to their values: Look for people who act with integrity, whether or not anyone is watching or expresses approval. Of course, no one likes to be mocked or criticized. But great role models know that not everyone is going to applaud them all the time.

They care about others: If heroism is defined by empathy and selflessness, look for role models who demonstrate these qualities. Seek mentors who believe that everyone matters and that heroic ventures are team efforts. **Success is seldom achieved alone,** and the best mentors appreciate and acknowledge the people who help out along the way.

They take risks: Heroic journeys are full of risks, so seek mentors who aren't afraid to screw up or fall flat on their faces in their own lives. Instead of giving up when things go south, the best role models are likely to say, "What can I do differently next time?"

They rejoice in the success of others: Some people look at life as a zero-sum game—if one person is winning, everyone else must be losing or falling behind. Seek role models who care more about improving the world than about their own standing in it.

Portrait of a Role Model

Once you have a mentor or role model (or several) in mind, take a few minutes to consider why you admire them. For this exercise, use a real person, either someone you know in your life or someone who's famous.

Across the top of a blank page, write down three of the qualities you most admire in that person. One-word answers work, such as courage, creativity, determination, kindness, love, or anything else you want.

Underneath each of the three qualities, describe an example of a time when your role model demonstrated that quality. For instance, if you chose Rosa Parks, you might write "determination" as one quality, and then describe how she stayed in her seat on the bus even though she knew she might get arrested.

Put your role model portrait up in your room or somewhere else you'll see it often. On tough or frustrating days, it will help **remind you of the heroic qualities** you most want to demonstrate no matter what challenges you face.

SEEKING MENTORS AND ROLE MODELS IN YOUR LIFE

Consider the heroic goal you identified in chapter 2, and think about the people in your life who might be most willing to help you achieve it. Make a list, and remember that you will probably need help from a range of people. Everyone has particular strengths and skills, and everyone has limitations. It's rare for one person to provide everything we need.

Like Malala's and Ethan's, your parents may already be important role models in your life, along with other family members. Certainly, these people can make ideal mentors, since they care about us deeply. Still, consider looking beyond your family as well. Seek people with different perspectives who have qualities you want to emulate.

Above all, look for people who are more interested in **forging connections between people** than in building barriers. "The basic rule of thumb is, what person is inclusive in their thinking versus exclusive?" says psychologist Scott Allison. "Who are the people who unite us, and who are the people who divide us?" People who have an "us-versus-them" take on the world encourage that type of thinking in others. They emphasize divisions and, sometimes, prejudice, such as believing those with more money are better or more deserving than others. Uniters, on the other hand, are natural peacemakers. They recognize the potential and value in all people.

Once you identify them, try to connect with your role models and mentors on a regular basis. This is straightforward if you live under the same roof, but if you don't, see if you can meet or talk with your role model once a week or once a month. Get creative if your role model is often busy. The important thing is that you set aside quality time to chat about your goals— and the bumps you're facing along the way. If your heroic vision isn't panning out the way you'd hoped, your role model might be able to help you brainstorm fresh approaches.

Then **remember that no one is perfect,** even our real-life heroes. Like everyone else, they'll make plenty of mistakes. They might be in a bad mood one day, or they might not have time to talk or respond swiftly to your emails and texts. That's one reason why we need numerous allies and mentors, since no one can be there all the time.

Irena Sendler died in 2008, but to this day, when Megan Felt faces challenges in life, she looks to Sendler's example. This remarkable woman's selflessness and friendship have changed her forever. Now a program director at the Lowell Milken Center for Unsung Heroes, Megan shares stories of heroes like Sendler with kids around the world.

In their own ways, the people we admire and choose as mentors and role models always change the world for the better. Once you've located your own, you'll be well on your way to becoming one of those world-changers yourself.

PROFILES IN COURAGE
Wong Siew Te

Growing up in Malaysia in the 1970s and 1980s, Wong Siew Te always felt a natural kinship with the furry, scaled, and feathered creatures around him. **If a bird fell out of a nest, Wong could be counted on to care for it.** He went to college in Taiwan with hopes of becoming a veterinarian, but he ended up embarking on a different journey—one that allowed him to help animals in ways he never expected.

After Wong went to the University of Montana to get his undergraduate degree in wildlife biology, he met an important mentor: the wildlife conservationist Christopher Servheen. Knowing that sun bears in Malaysia were in danger, Servheen was looking for a student who would be willing to do research on sun bears and their life in the wild. Wong answered the call, telling Servheen, "I'm your man!"

With Servheen's support, Wong traveled to Malaysia and started spending many hours a day studying sun bears. As he got to know the bears, he realized the full extent of the danger they face. The logging industry in Malaysia clears acres and acres of rainforest for timber, decimating the shaded groves where the bears live. Poachers also kill the bears and sell them to people who use their body parts in traditional medicine.

The more time Wong spent around the sun bears, **the more he realized he wanted to safeguard their lives and habitats.** In 2008, he founded a nonprofit organization called the Bornean Sun Bear Conservation Centre— the world's first conservation group dedicated to sun bears. At any given time, a few dozen rescued sun bears live at the center. Many are brought in when poachers kill their parents or when careless owners leave them locked in tiny cages.

Each day, the bears at the center roam the forested grounds, climbing trees and building nests. If and when the animals are ready, the center sends them back into the wild. The center also trains local conservation specialists and educates young students about the sun bears' plight.

In 2017, Wong received a CNN Heroes award, and he told a reporter: "Sun bears became part of my family. When they're endangered, I care for them. When they are in trouble, I speak for them."

5 OVERCOMING OBSTACLES MEANS STANDING OUT

Pursuing a heroic goal takes determination and courage. As we know from the hero's journey, it means overcoming a range of obstacles and tests—and one common obstacle is the disapproval of others. If mentors and allies are the ones who encourage and help us, there are always others who don't or won't.

No matter what we're doing, **standing out always takes serious gumption.** People and society often encourage us to "Be unique!" and "Be yourself!" That is, until others become uncomfortable with what we're up to or the way we choose to express ourselves. Then people tell us to "Play along!" and "Don't rock the boat!"

Researchers have found that people with strong moral beliefs are more likely to risk voicing an opinion that differs from the norm. If people try to put you down for airing these kinds of views, simply explain, as clearly and honestly as you can, why you're doing what you're doing. Always try to be courteous and polite; some people will disagree with you, and that's to be expected.

As challenges and obstacles arise, use them to clarify for yourself why your heroic goal is important and what good you hope to achieve. Review the lists of heroic qualities in chapter 1, and perhaps even adjust the goal you defined in chapter 2. The clearer and more confident you feel about what you're doing and why, the easier it will be to **stand up to those who doubt you or disagree.**

To all potential heroes, author Dave Rendall poses this question: "Over time, the people we admire—Gandhi, Martin Luther King, Abe Lincoln, they sacrificed for what they believed in. Who do you admire? Is it people who stayed out of the way and made sure never to endure any discomfort?"

WHAT IT MEANS TO BE A FREAK

Dave Rendall is the author of *The Freak Factor: Discovering Uniqueness by Flaunting Weakness*. His message? Don't feel ashamed about standing out from the crowd—take pride in it.

Dave knows what he's talking about. Early in life, he got used to staring at the tops of people's heads. By the time he was in high school, he was more than six

feet tall, and he was so skinny that people called him "Twiggy." But his stature wasn't the only thing that set him apart from his classmates. Growing up in the 1980s, he had a hard time containing his enthusiasm—he'd bubble over with thoughts or opinions he just had to share, and then he'd get in trouble for interrupting or talking over others. The way he saw it, his parents and teachers had one main goal: to get him to sit at his desk and shut up.

When Dave took an out-of-the box approach with his schoolwork, he got crucified. "I wrote a paper, and every word started with the letter B. I got an F on that assignment," he remembers. "People told me, 'Dave, you're never going to amount to anything.'" Other kids started picking on him and shunning him. They called him a freak and much worse on a regular basis.

For years, Dave believed what the world seemed to be telling him—that he was defective, the human equivalent of a two-legged stool. Not until much later, when he was working and living independently, did his outlook change. To his surprise, he started realizing that **the very qualities people used to criticize—his animated personality and gift of gab—were helping him get ahead.** After he graduated from college, a group he was part of needed a person to give a speech. Someone said, "Dave will do it!"

Dave stepped up to the challenge and discovered that he truly loved teaching and speaking. Talking to people gave him a burst of energy and excitement that didn't fade. The best part was that no hall monitor lurked over his shoulder, telling him to keep his voice down. "I started seeing that my weaknesses were strengths," Dave says, "and that there was hope for using them as opposed to having to stifle them for the rest of my life."

Out of the Box

These days, Dave makes a living by celebrating his own inner freakdom and encouraging others to do the same, speaking to audiences in the United States and around the world.

If you've ever been told to "get with the program," or if you're used to getting funny looks, Dave's struggles might sound familiar. The good news, as he can attest, is that **embracing what makes you different** can help you succeed and even lead you to your own heroic calling.

BE A FREAK FOR A DAY

Most of us are not born with the self-confidence to stand up and stand out. It's a skill we learn over time by overcoming obstacles and working to achieve heroic goals. "Heroism requires us to act when no one else is acting," Dave Rendall says. "Stand up when everyone else is sitting down."

In other words, heroes need to be able to tune out sideways glances, critical voices, and snickers so they can act effectively on others' behalf. Taking a moral stand or extending a helping hand may not always be met with approval, so you need to **be strong** to proceed anyway.

In itself, being different is not bad. Dave Rendall's teachers quickly labeled him a troublemaker, but he didn't mean to cause trouble or harm. He didn't break windows or sling insults. His energy and interests just didn't fit classroom expectations.

Intentions, then, make a big difference. The critical difference, in fact. People who enjoy making a scene or sowing pointless strife are not "helping" or pursuing a heroic goal. This is different from those who express themselves in a positive way in order to change something that is harmful. If, or when, people accuse you of being a "troublemaker," consider your motivations and make sure your intentions are helpful. Are you voicing an unheard perspective, developing your talents, or standing up for someone who's not getting a fair chance? Make sure your actions align with your deepest values.

You can also practice feeling more at home with being different. Hero experts recommend experimenting with your own quirkiness just for the fun of it, which will help you get comfortable with standing out when it really counts. "Start out being different in small harmless ways, so you can see it's okay to be different," says psychologist Scott Allison. "Wear the orange shoes when no one else is wearing the orange shoes." Dave Rendall, who loves look-at-me colors like neon pink, heartily agrees.

Here are some suggestions for how to be a freak for a day:

- Wear a turban of fruit on your head, like the Chiquita Banana lady, then hand out fruit to anyone who wants some.
- Talk only in the low, breathy voice of Darth Vader from *Star Wars*. When you meet someone, rasp out, "I am your father."
- Wear a pair of giant clown shoes.
- Stand in front of the mall and hand out little homemade care packages of candy, stickers, or wind-up toys. Tell people you're doing good by giving away "mall survival kits."

- Shave your head. If you want, do it to raise awareness about cancer and ask people if they'd like to donate to cancer research—then donate the money you get!

If you can convince your whole class to throw a "Be a Freak for a Day" party, you'll get to test your stand-alone mettle while other people are testing theirs. It's a chance for everyone to be silly in their own way and see that it's okay. **You get bonus points if you can get your teacher or principal to participate.** The point is to celebrate uniqueness, instead of trying to get everyone to conform.

Afterward, talk about the experience with friends. What did it feel like to do something (or say something, or wear something) that you usually don't? Was it harder than you thought or easier to **overcome your fear of standing out?** Do you think you might be able to do it again if the situation called for it—even if it still feels uncomfortable?

Dave Rendall is a prime example of what you can achieve if you accept your own so-called freakishness. He's on the road hundreds of days a year sharing his message of inclusion, bravery, and self-acceptance, and changing thousands of lives—all while rocking his signature pink shoes. "We make difference a problem, but it doesn't have to be," he says. In choosing the right times to defy what everyone else expects of you, you make room for your own inner hero to emerge.

FREAK

PROFILES IN COURAGE
Dominique Moceanu

When she was just fourteen years old, gymnast Dominique Moceanu took the 1996 Summer Olympic Games by storm, back-flipping and twisting her way to the gold medal with her American teammates. The Olympics in Atlanta ushered in a flurry of excitement—among other things, Dominique got to party at Planet Hollywood with celebrities Bruce Willis and Demi Moore.

But behind the scenes, Dominique's day-to-day life as a gymnast had become harder and harder to bear. During the Olympics, Dominique competed with a two-inch-long stress fracture in her right leg, which was brought on by coaches who had overtrained her for months. On a regular basis, Dominique's coaches ridiculed her and the other female gymnasts, calling them fat and lazy. The coaches pushed the girls to train even when they were hurt, which led to Dominique's problem.

Dominique always felt that the way female gymnasts were treated was wrong—that it amounted to abuse. So, after her gymnastics career ended, she was determined to change things. In 2008, Dominique appeared on TV to tell her story, and in 2012, she wrote a book called *Off Balance*. Dominique called for fairer treatment of athletes, but not everyone was receptive to this message. At times, she felt like an outcast for speaking up. "It's very lonely when you don't have public support," Dominique says. "People start attacking you, saying, 'What you're saying is not true.'"

Despite the obstacles she faced, Dominique refused to back down. She persevered in the hopes that future gymnasts wouldn't suffer the same treatment she had. In 2017, her efforts were finally rewarded: An in-depth report on abuse inside USA Gymnastics advised that anyone witnessing athlete mistreatment be required to report it to authorities. Despite the criticism she's endured, **Dominique doesn't regret speaking up.** "I knew in my heart that if I did the right thing," she says, "the rest would just fall into place."

6 HEROES GET SCHOOLED

It's 9:53 am, and the bell has just rung to start class at Wilson High School in Portland, Oregon. But this is hardly your average classroom. Instead of desks, more than twenty yoga mats are arranged in a circle on the floor. And instead of a parade of tacked-up "A" papers, the walls feature a colorful forest mural the students designed and painted themselves.

"All right, let's start in child pose," says Allyson Copacino, one of the teachers. The students wrap up their conversations, tuck their knees under their torsos, and let their foreheads rest on the mats. "Take a long deep breath in through your nose, and fill your entire body with breath," Copacino continues. "Exhale and let it all go." As the meditation progresses, she encourages the students to **turn their thoughts to their future hopes.** "Maybe think about one thing you want to try to cultivate," she says. "What do you want to bring into your life?"

The students in this classroom are mat-sitting pioneers, participants in the first for-credit high school mindfulness class in the country. Over the course of the semester, they've practiced meditating for longer periods of time, which means learning how to **focus their attention, quiet their minds,** and be alert to whatever's happening in the moment. When distracting thoughts flit through their awareness, they return their attention to the present and the gentle, in-and-out motion of their breath.

Very few schools have tried squeezing a mindfulness class between social studies and study hall, but Wilson High School isn't alone in thinking education should involve more than mastering the "three Rs." Around the world, fired-up educators are introducing students to principles they can use to realize their heroic potential. They're teaching skills no standardized test can measure, like the power to pay close attention, the ability to empathize with others, and the courage to be the lone voice of reason in a crowd.

Some people don't see how concepts like mindfulness and empathy are useful. They feel students should focus on writing essays, memorizing the periodic table, and learning history. To succeed at life, however, we need more than textbook knowledge. There's a connection between paying attention in the moment, feeling empathy for others, and being creative enough to overcome obstacles and find effective solutions.

Research suggests that improving our present-moment awareness makes us better at understanding what others are thinking and feeling. That knowledge, in turn, can motivate us to help them. In one study, people who'd gotten eight weeks of meditation training were several times more likely than nonmeditators to help a person on crutches—the kind of everyday heroism psychologist Philip Zimbardo encourages.

In addition, more than 90 percent of students who took Wilson High School's Mindful Studies class reported better mental and emotional well-being, which is no small contributor to heroic success. **It's much easier to care about how others are doing when you're feeling good yourself.** "This class has helped me to be happier and more accepting toward myself and others," one teen said afterward. "I'm learning skills here that will last me a lifetime."

PRACTICING MINDFULNESS

You don't need a teacher or a class to improve mindfulness or to develop your present-moment awareness. All you need is practice. Do this meditation whenever you can for just ten minutes. You can set a timer (like on your cell phone) so you know when the time is up.

1. Sit comfortably in any position—it can be the edge of your bed, a yoga mat, or even a hard floor. If you're in a chair, make sure both of your feet are flat on the floor. If you're on the floor, sit cross-legged, with your feet tucked under your calves.

2. Close your eyes and pay attention to the sensation of air traveling in and out through your nose. Does it feel cool? Warm? Dry? Does your chest expand and contract as you breathe, or does it mostly remain still?

3. **Continue focusing as best you can on your breath.** If your focus drifts—and it probably will, as you think about what you're doing that day or the soft pretzel you'd love to eat—don't beat yourself up about it. Simply notice that it's happened, and refocus on the breath as it moves in and out.

And that's it! The only goal is to focus on your breath, without thinking about anything else, for ten minutes. If you've never meditated before, consider doing this practice for ten minutes a day every day for a week.

At the end of the week, notice if you feel any different. Are you better at paying attention to what's happening in the moment? Do you feel calmer when an unexpected situation confronts you? Write a journal entry about your experience and what you notice.

LEARNING SKILLS TO TACKLE TRIALS

Once we name a heroic goal, success means solving whatever tests and problems arise. These tests are not the kind you take in school, and with a few exceptions like Wilson High School, what you need to learn isn't taught in a classroom. Rather, to be a hero, you have to take charge of your own heroic education and learn whatever you need to.

The first thing this requires is what psychologist Carol Dweck calls a "growth mindset." When we have a "fixed mindset," we believe our skills and abilities are basically set in stone. So, if we fail a math test once, we believe that we'll *always* be bad at math; if we get a few "nos" when we ask people for money to support a cause, we decide we're just no good at fundraising. A growth mindset takes the opposite perspective. If we fail at something the first time (or the second or third time), that shows where we need to improve, and if we invest enough time and effort, we can learn the skills we need.

The **growth mindset is necessary** when we hit roadblocks on our heroic quest. This mindset doesn't mean believing that, through practice, we'll eventually become "the best" or "experts" at something. We may never get straight As in math or become Olympic athletes. But we *can* believe in our ability to improve: to brainstorm approaches, learn what we need, and get additional help until we succeed.

The connection between learning and helping others is most direct when it comes to life-saving skills. Anyone can become CPR certified, and if you are, then you'll know what to do if, say, a diner in a restaurant is choking. Many other basic life skills—swimming, balancing a checkbook, driving a car, public speaking—might be needed to help others, and all these can be learned and improved through practice long before you have a heroic goal that calls for them.

Be Ready for Action

Philip Zimbardo's Heroic Imagination Project (HIP) teaches other ways of sharpening the tools in your heroic arsenal. In places as diverse as China, Poland, and the United States, the Heroic Imagination Project teaches kids how to liberate their inner hero by practicing how to recognize problems and then step forward or speak out to help.

One way HIP prepares young people to be heroes is by teaching them to avoid the bystander effect. Researchers have found that, if only one person is nearby when someone gets attacked or becomes ill, then that person will often rush to help the person in trouble. On the other hand, if a *group* of people is standing nearby, then each individual observer is very unlikely to help. Why is this? **Humans are a social species,** and we pay a lot of attention to how others behave. If we see other people ignoring a victim, we might follow suit, or we might assume that someone else will step in to help.

To help students understand how the bystander effect can show up in real life, HIP teachers encourage them to imagine that they're walking home from school, and they see someone lying on the sidewalk. Other people pass by without helping. As a class, the students discuss what they think they would do. Would they stop and try to figure out what was wrong? Or would they walk on by or even speed up? Then they watch a video that shows the bystander effect in action in real life. A man sprawls on the steps of a public building, looking as if he is about to faint or have a heart attack, and person after person walks past without breaking stride.

Later on, students learn how to overcome the natural impulse to hang back. When a problem arises, instead of reacting instantly, they practice pausing and taking a few seconds to gather their thoughts. They might ask themselves, "Am I being a bystander?" Teachers introduce the concept of **"diffusion of responsibility."** This refers to how, when more people are around, we are more likely to assume someone else will take charge of a situation. Then again, if everyone thinks this, it's possible *no one* will do anything—and remembering this can spur you to act. The motto "Be the first!" is a reminder that, if someone needs help, you should try to help in whatever way you can—and also strive to enlist the support of other people.

TAKE CHARGE OF YOUR HEROIC EDUCATION

Of course, this kind of heroic education is easiest to learn from teachers, mentors, and organizations like the Heroic Imagination Project. If you feel inspired, you could seek out organizations like Peace in Schools and Learning to Breathe, which have their own mindfulness curricula, or you could ask your school or teachers to consider including some of these lessons in your school.

However, you can also **take charge of your own heroic education.** Try this HIP-inspired thought experiment, either on your own or with some friends: Think back on a time when you opted to do the right thing or help someone who was in need. Then, think

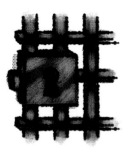

of a time when you *did not* act selflessly to help. Now compare the two scenarios. What do you think encouraged you to help in the first situation, and what held you back from helping in the second? Most importantly, what do you think you could do in the future to get past feeling reluctant to act?

The point of this isn't to feel bad over mistakes and times when we didn't act. Instead, we learn from these experiences so we can do better next time. As one student wrote after completing an HIP course, "If someone needs help, we must break the barriers of conformism and be the first to help, because **a little bit of assistance can make all the difference.**"

No matter what real-life situations we face or what tactics we use to approach them, the foundation of any heroic response rests on paying close attention to what's going on. As they still their minds in a light-filled classroom sanctuary, that's exactly what Wilson High School students are learning to do.

"Just rest the attention here in the present moment," says Caverly Morgan, the class's coteacher, as students prepare for a final ten-minute sitting meditation. "There's nothing you have to do. Nowhere you have to go."

That kind of self-control and openness to whatever happens might not always land you A-plus grades in school, but it *can* clear the way for you to overcome obstacles and realize your highest heroic potential.

PROFILES IN COURAGE
Philip Zimbardo

As a street-smart kid growing up in New York City's Bronx borough, Philip Zimbardo witnessed things like fights and gang activity on a regular basis. He thought a lot about what was going on around him, and eventually, he started asking himself an important question. **Why did some kids in his neighborhood go on to become successful,** with educations, steady jobs, and lofty values, while others got sucked into lives of violence and crime?

That curiosity led him to study psychology—which, boiled down to the most basic terms, is the science of why people think and behave as they do. As a psychology professor at Stanford University, he designed a study that has since become infamous and controversial: the Stanford Prison Experiment, a simulation of real jail conditions. He gathered a group of regular college students and told some of them they would be "prisoners" and others they would be "guards."

Yet before too long, the situation spiraled out of control, with the guards abusing the prisoners in horrific ways. "Guards" prevented "prisoners" from using the bathroom, forcing them to use plastic buckets instead. They took the prisoners' mattresses and wouldn't let them sleep for more than a few hours at a time. After just six days, the guards' power trip got so out of hand that Zimbardo decided he had to cancel the experiment. (Recent reporting has revealed that some of the guards were coached to act tough, but Zimbardo argues that their sadistic behavior went way beyond toughness.)

For decades after the prison experiment, Zimbardo wrestled with what made regular, ordinary people behave badly in certain situations. But the more he thought about it, the more he realized there was a flip side. If normal people could become their worst selves under certain conditions, couldn't they also become their best selves under different conditions?

Zimbardo decided to turn his attention to heroes instead, people who rise above their dark impulses. A few years ago, he created the nonprofit Heroic Imagination Project (HIP) in his hometown of San Francisco. Not only would HIP support research about heroism, it would teach people—kids and adults alike—how to discover their most heroic selves.

Since then, **HIP has taught "heroes-in-training"** how bad situations can influence people to act in ways that do not reflect their morals and values—like in the Stanford Prison Experiment—and how to act in ways that better reflect their true selves.

Now in his eighties, Zimbardo still travels around the globe to impart his hero-building message. He likes to sport a Superman-inspired shirt with a big letter Z on the front, and he never gets tired of urging people to get in touch with their inner hero.

7 PASSING THE TEST

Of course, no matter how much we study, plan, and prepare, we can't know what tests and obstacles we'll face in life. And no matter how much help we get from mentors and allies, overcoming obstacles is still hard. As you pursue your heroic goal and embark on your hero's journey, try not to get discouraged if troubles seem tougher and more complicated than you thought. Just remember: Learning how to solve problems by recognizing the most effective approach in each particular situation is the key to success. **Real-life heroes don't just jump into action blindly.** They think carefully about how to pass each test.

For instance, consider Juliana Davis. In 2014, when Juliana was a senior at Swartz Creek High School in Michigan, she took a leadership course. In class, her classmates started discussing some of the vile things students at the school were saying about others on a cell phone app called After School. Users could post anything they wanted on the app without using their names, and under the cloak of anonymity, they felt free to launch blistering attacks. Some posts made fun of gay students, while others threatened physical violence or goaded students to kill themselves.

The more Juliana learned about what people were saying on the app, the more horrified she became. "I saw a girl crying in the hall, and someone told me it was because of the app," Juliana says. "At that point, I knew something needed to be done."

So Juliana decided to take action to **protect people from getting hurt.** She knew she didn't want to engage with bullies directly, by confronting or attacking them. That would only turn her into a target. So, instead of focusing on the students who were being mean, she decided to try to shut down the app itself.

Juliana put together an online petition on the website change.org, asking Apple to remove After School from its online store. That way, the anonymous bullies would no longer have a place to air their hate. People who supported Juliana's efforts passed the link along to others. Before long, people she didn't know— some from states she'd never even visited—were signing the petition.

But Juliana knew other apps could end up playing the same role if After School disappeared, so she started another petition with her friend Elizabeth Long. This one urged sellers like Apple to enforce stronger antibullying standards on all anonymous posting

What's Your Name?

apps. "These apps have the potential to be extremely dangerous," Juliana and Elizabeth wrote. "With no way to identify posters, it makes it incredibly difficult for schools and law enforcement to find people who post threats, or whose bullying comments lead to violence or suicide."

Juliana knew that starting a petition involved risk. Because she was speaking up and trying to police the anonymous apps, she was scared other kids at her school might attack her. "That was my biggest fear," she says. "I wouldn't let myself download the [After School] app because I didn't want to see what people were saying, if they were saying anything."

In the end, after more than a thousand people signed Juliana's first petition, Apple removed the program from its store. A little while later, the app returned, but in a different form. The creators made a number of changes to try to curb bullying, including blocking posts where posters told others to hurt themselves. Ultimately, Juliana's efforts to thwart bullying on the After School app were rewarded.

Juliana says she's proud of what she accomplished, and she'd face the fear and uncertainty all over again if she had to. "I'd like to think that **what my peers and I did caused positive changes,** and I could never want to take back something like that."

It took courage for Juliana to stand up for what she believed in. She took a risk by speaking out on behalf of those who were being bullied on the app. But it was a calculated risk. Juliana thought carefully about her actions, both to minimize any danger to herself and to find the most effective solution.

This chapter offers advice for figuring out how to solve problems in the most effective way, as Juliana did, so that your heroic efforts have the best chance of success.

DARE GREATLY, BUT SHREWDLY: A THREE-PART STRATEGY

One common misconception from comic-book superheroes is that heroes use all their force to impose the right solution, no matter what. Villains are vanquished even if whole cities get leveled. In real life, we can't act like this. **We have to consider the needs and concerns of everyone involved** and come up with the best, most effective solution for all: given the particular situation or problem, given what we want, and given what others want.

When it comes to heroic actions, there's often a fine line between daring success and foolhardy mistakes. If Juliana had handled her situation differently—by confronting bullies in the school hallway, for instance, or hurling insults online—she might have created even *more* problems, not just for herself, but for the students who were being bullied. What made the difference was

how Juliana decided to tackle the bullying problem and how she handled herself in the process.

These are key skills you need no matter what your goals. They apply in emergency situations—like Graceanne Andreessen's, when you must act quickly and put yourself at physical risk—and they also apply in nonemergency situations like Juliana's, when your goal is to speak up or persuade people to change their behavior. Even when our aim is to help others, **"self-preservation is important,"** says psychologist Scott Allison.

The ability to interpret a situation quickly and accurately is what experts call "situational awareness." When you have well-honed situational awareness, you can figure out exactly what's going on and take the shrewdest, least foolhardy action possible—within seconds, if you need to.

To become situationally aware, you need to hone three abilities: the capacity to take in what's happening around you, a healthy understanding of your strengths and weaknesses, and anticipating how others may respond to the situation or to what you might do.

Present-Moment Awareness: Understanding What's Happening around You

To help someone or to fix a problem, we first have to fully understand what's going on. That may sound simple or obvious, but it can be surprisingly easy to lose sight of what matters or to assume our unique perspective amounts to the whole picture. When that happens, we might miss, or misinterpret, what's actually going on.

The best way to combat this tendency is to train your attention on what's happening right now, not what happened yesterday or what could happen eight minutes from now. You can practice this kind of alertness any time by hitting the "mental pause button," as the Heroic Imagination Project teaches. This means, at any moment, and wherever you are, pausing, taking a deep breath, and paying attention to what's in front of you. Do you notice any unusual sights or sounds? Does anything around you seem unexpected or off-kilter? What do you feel? Resist the temptation to shut out anything that's surprising or unsettling; simply let it all in.

This is a way of grounding yourself in the moment, and it's especially important to pause when something happens and you feel the urge to react instantly. Let's say you overhear someone saying something mean about a disabled student. By hitting your "pause button," you give yourself time to assess the situation so you can take effective and appropriate action. You might ask yourself a series of questions: "Who is talking, and who are they talking to? Are they actively hurting someone or speaking quietly, thinking no one hears? In other words, is someone being mocked or bullied publicly, or are kids being inappropriate in private?"

The nature of the problem often determines the best, most effective response.

Know Yourself: Understanding Your Strengths and Weaknesses

Once you've taken time to assess a situation, realistically consider what you can and can't do to improve it. While you may wish you had superhero qualities like invincibility or the strength of a squad of T. rexes, pretending you have them could be a catastrophic mistake. Be aware of your own strengths and weaknesses in any given situation to decide how to help.

Unlike superheroes, who tend to use one or two superpowers to solve all problems, real-life heroes have to be flexible and adapt to what the moment calls for. For instance, if you see someone getting robbed at a bus stop, what should you do? Like Spider-Man, you may want to tackle and subdue the assailant, wrapping them up for police to find. But you're not Spider-Man, and fighting muggers is probably the *last* thing you should do. Yet you can help in other ways: You can attend to the person who is hurt, call the police, alert others to the crime, and perhaps make an audio or video recording to help identify the thief later.

Heroic intentions alone aren't always enough. A lot of people have genuinely good intentions, but they act before fully considering their actions: They may rush and do the wrong thing because they didn't check with people who were already involved. They might attempt actions they don't have the authority, expertise, or skills to pull off. And they may not consider the potential, unintended harm their actions might cause. If you rushed into a blazing home to save someone without any fire protection, you could get trapped and burned yourself—and you'd make the firefighters' job that much harder because now they'd have to rescue you, too.

When your action plan lines up with your true strengths, **your chances of success** are much greater For instance, to help stop online bullying, Juliana Davis used her writing skills to start a petition to protest the app that was causing the problem. With this petition, she got the support of thousands of people, which helped her antibullying efforts succeed. Similarly, when Ethan King decided to start a charity donating soccer balls to poor villages, he knew that his enthusiasm was boundless, but his capabilities were limited. He was only ten. So he enlisted his father and other trusted adults to help him get his organization started.

In fact, many times, solving problems effectively means getting help. Sure, it's fun to picture ourselves as the conquering hero, saving the day alone, but that's rarely how real life works. Real heroes consult mentors and gather allies, which I discuss further in chapter 9.

At other times, the only way to solve a problem is to have the necessary skills or training. If you don't know CPR or how to do the Heimlich maneuver, you can't use them. But you can learn, and if you do, then you *will* be equipped to intervene in a life-or-death situation. Running a nonprofit means you need to manage its finances and file taxes correctly. So to start a nonprofit, you need to learn those skills—or ask someone else for help. Remember, learning skills is all part of the hero's journey. In stories, that's the point of tests and obstacles; they teach the hero the skills he or she needs to complete the mission.

In particular, in emergency situations, **never try to save the day alone** unless there really is no other option. Always try to get help. "Safety is number one," says David Nance, president of the SABRE Personal Safety Academy. "Taking care of yourself first and calling for help are probably your best bets."

Considering Others: Anticipating How Others Will Respond

By definition, any action you take to help others will impact and affect those people. And it will probably affect other people, too. Do you know how everyone will react to what you want to do? Are you sure your actions will have the impact you want? In particular, who might disagree with you, and for what reason? These are questions you should consider before taking action.

As we know from mythic stories, some people support the hero and others don't. These story antagonists resist or defy the hero. Usually, they like things the way they are and don't want to do anything differently. If you know that someone might be upset by your efforts to help, consider if there are ways to solve the problem that address their concerns. **Could you act or handle yourself differently and still get what you want?**

In the late 1980s, Neto Villarreal found a powerful way to do this when he played on his high school football team in Marsing, Idaho. When Neto and other Latino players made mistakes on the field, spectators often lobbed racist insults like "Stupid Mexican!" This was hurtful, and after a while, Neto decided to take a stand. He and some of the other Latino players decided that if they couldn't play football without hearing racial taunts, they would stop playing football altogether.

They didn't *want* to stop playing football. Their goal was to stop what they considered rude and insulting behavior. But how could they communicate this to the entire school, and their whole community, without making the situation worse? Neto decided to describe their plan to school district officials at a school board meeting. The school superintendent approved, and at the next football game, a member of the Marsing High School student council announced over the loudspeaker that anyone who yelled racist insults in the future would be kicked out of games. Neto was afraid of how the crowd might respond, but spectators at the stadium erupted in a roar of cheering agreement. With this show of community respect and support, Neto and his friends happily took the field with the rest of their teammates.

REHEARSING COURAGEOUS CONVERSATIONS

Taking a heroic stand can be tricky. We want to intervene courageously and improve a situation, not act in ways that make things worse or cause more trouble. **Figuring out the right balance is hard,** and what's best can be different in every situation. Not only does it help to think about all the possible outcomes, even extreme and unlikely ones, but it can help to rehearse difficult situations or conversations in advance. This can boost your confidence when the moment to speak up or to make your case arrives.

For instance, what if you wanted to talk to an adult about racist insults *you* heard other kids flinging around in the hallways at school? Who should you approach, and what should you say? There's no perfect answer, and even having this type of conversation might seem intimidating.

So practice. You'd never set foot on stage without rehearsing your lines dozens of times, or play in a soccer game without practicing dribbling and corner kicks over and over. Similarly, you **strengthen your chances of success** when you practice difficult conversations.

Many heroic goals involve confronting others, speaking up, or doing things that are unfamiliar or difficult. If you face a courageous conversation, go over each step of your plan in your mind. Write it down, if that helps. Then talk it through with a friend, mentor, ally, or trusted adult. Keep rehearsing what you'll say, and changing and adjusting the plan as necessary, until you feel good about your chances of success *and* your ability to carry it out.

Here is a three-step plan:

1. Name or list what your goals are, who you need to talk with, and what you need to say. Define what it is you are asking for; make sure your request is clear. Do you want the other person just to agree with you, or do you want to ask them to do something? Be specific about what you want from the conversation, or how to define "success."

2. Enlist a friend and role-play the encounter. Obviously, you would play yourself, and your friend would play the other person. Your friend

should act as much like the other person as possible. Try different approaches: Explain the problem and ask for what you want in various ways. While still being realistic, your friend could modify their reaction: open and understanding one time, and less so the next time. Don't be afraid to improvise.

3. When you're done, or as you go, debrief each other. Did anything happen that surprised you? Describe how you felt, and ask your friend to grade your performance. Was it easier or harder to speak up than you'd imagined? Most importantly, do you feel you can express yourself in a way that reflects your goal and your best self?

The truth is, no heroic goal is ever risk-free. One of the things that defines heroes is that they are willing to take risks. Smart heroes dare greatly, but they also *minimize* the risks they face. And that might be the best way to think about this chapter's advice. **Real-life heroes take risks all the time,** but they aren't careless. Firefighters enter burning buildings only after months and years of hard training, and they do so wearing full-body fireproof gear. Juliana Davis and Neto Villarreal both took a stand for respecting others, and they did so in measured, well-thought-out ways that produced positive change. Successful heroism takes more than just courage—it also takes awareness, training, practice, and planning.

A SHREWD HERO'S TOOL KIT

To summarize the advice in this chapter, **keep these points in mind as you decide what heroic actions to take:**

- When problems arise, hit the mental pause button. Make sure you understand what's happening before reacting.
- Stay calm on the outside—don't sling threats or insults.
- Know your strengths, weaknesses, and role in each situation.
- Get the training you need—ideally, before you need it.
- Get help and delegate as needed.
- Consider how everyone involved may respond to you.
- Rehearse, rehearse, rehearse difficult conversations and encounters.

PROFILES IN COURAGE
Paige Dayal

In 2012, fourteen-year-old Paige Dayal of Newmarket, Canada, was browsing the internet one day when she saw an alarming post on Tumblr. The poster, named Luke, was someone she didn't know in real life, but he had written that everyone hated him and he didn't have a friend in the world. The post was gloomy, and the comments underneath it were worse—online bullies were telling Luke to go ahead and commit suicide. Paige feared Luke was going to hurt himself.

Paige couldn't stop thinking about Luke's post, so she decided to enlist the help of her mom, Laura Stevenson, a therapist who assists troubled kids. Stevenson called the local police station, but they said **they couldn't do anything** about someone making posts online.

As the minutes ticked by and no further posts from Luke appeared, Paige grew frantic. A few online search queries revealed that Luke lived in a small town near the city of Bath

in England. At Paige's insistence, her mom contacted a policeman near Bath. The officer thanked them for calling and promised to check on Luke as soon as possible.

A couple of hours later, a new post from Luke popped up on Tumblr: "I am so grateful to the girl who rang the police," the post read. "Seriously I LOVE YOU." Thanks to Paige and her mother's intervention, a policeman had come to Luke's house after he had taken some pills. Now he was at the hospital with his parents and getting help.

Overcome by happiness and relief, Paige did a happy dance right there. Halfway around the world, she and her mom had managed to pull off an incredible rescue. What's more, it didn't require a private jet or CPR training. Just attention, compassion, and perseverance until they found someone who listened.

8 TRANSFORM PAIN INTO HEROIC PURPOSE

Antoinette Tuff had faced pain and struggle head-on for as long as she could remember. Her father left her family when she was two years old, and when she was ten, her mother got sick with cancer. Since 2008, Tuff had worked as a bookkeeper at Georgia's Ronald E. McNair Discovery Learning Academy, but much of her salary went toward providing care for her disabled son, Derrick. On top of that, in 2012, her husband of thirty-three years left her.

But things got worse on the afternoon of August 20, 2013. Soon after Tuff, then forty-six, sat down at her desk in the front office that day, a young man—hardly older than a high school student—rushed in. He was dressed in black from head to toe, and his eyes blazed, like there was some demon inside him that was raging to get out.

He started waving an AK-47 assault rifle and firing at the ground. "This is not a joke! This is real," he yelled. "We are all going to die today!"

Tuff's heart thumped double-time, and her

bladder threatened to burst. But she managed to stay calm on the surface and keep talking to the gunman. Eventually, the man, whose name was Michael Hill, began to let his guard down. He had gone off his medication a while ago, he told Tuff; he wasn't feeling stable. "I just want to die," Hill told her.

Tuff sensed that Hill's deep pain was genuine. She knew life could seem impossible enough to make you want to lash out or just give up entirely. So she decided to share her own struggles with the would-be shooter. "You know, I tried to commit suicide last year after my husband left me," she said. "But look at me now. I'm still working and everything is okay. It's gonna be all right, sweetheart. I just want you to know that I love you, though, okay?"

It was Tuff's **compassion and reassurance** that prompted Michael Hill to set down his gun. Tuff's quick thinking kept every student at McNair safe that day. "The reason I was able to show Michael Hill compassion . . . is because, in a way, I was Michael Hill," Tuff later wrote. "I understood the torment of having no place to go and no one to turn to, because I felt those very things myself."

THE FINAL ORDEAL IS OUR BIGGEST CHALLENGE

In hero's journey terms, Antoinette Tuff's encounter with Michael Hill corresponds to the final ordeal every mythic hero must face. Tuff literally faced death that day and survived, and death is typically the climactic danger in heroic stories. More importantly, to convince Hill to put aside his plans, Tuff had to confront the full depths of her own pain and transform it into empathy and compassion. This is what it means to say that, in the mythic hero's journey, the hero is transformed by the final ordeal and receives a "reward" that saves the day.

In this case, by choosing to face and expose her own pain, Tuff kept all the kids at McNair safe from a raging young man who had pledged to kill them. If she had not met the heroic challenge that was thrust upon her, who knows what would have happened that day?

Our lives are not stories. There's no telling when, in the course of our own heroic journeys, we will face our final ordeal. We may not even recognize this moment until later. Certainly, whatever happens, our lives continue afterward. We may even face multiple final ordeals. However it unfolds, the final ordeal involves confronting our own pain, difficulties, and struggles and **transforming them into power, love, and purpose.**

Everyone wrestles with pain and grief. You can probably think of times when you've struggled at school, deflected taunts and insults, fallen short of your goals, or lost someone you care about. You may have even felt as hopeless as Antoinette Tuff or Michael Hill.

The message of the hero's journey is that the seeds of strength and redemption exist within even the greatest pain. When you push through tough times and stay committed to what you believe in, **you can emerge with new wisdom, understanding, and compassion.** In fact, the hard things you go through can give you a burning desire to help others and fix problems. They can spur you to heroic acts.

It might seem counterintuitive that hard times can fuel our concern for others. But as with Antoinette Tuff, sometimes pain causes us to feel a kinship with other people going through similar difficulties. That kinship can motivate us to reach out because we don't want others to suffer the same way we have.

A number of years ago, University of Massachusetts psychologist Ervin Staub and his team studied the relationship of altruism to personal pain. They asked a group of people if they would help victims of a 2004 tsunami in Southeast Asia, and they found that people who had been through serious past difficulties were more likely to agree to collect money for tsunami victims. Staub called this compassionate response "altruism born of suffering." There's no question that Antoinette Tuff displayed altruism born of suffering when she drew on her own painful past to comfort Michael Hill.

TRANSFORMING YOUR OWN PAIN

How can you transform your own hard times into a sense of strength and purpose in your heroic quest? That's not easy to answer. The reason this stage is called the final ordeal is because it represents one of the most difficult experiences we'll ever have.

First off, to be clear, when you do go through something tough, it's totally normal to be angry and say to yourself, "This sucks!" It can be hard to find compassion for others when our own wounds are still fresh. Give yourself time to heal. When you feel ready, **turn your thoughts to others** and ask, "How many other people out there have gone through something like this? And is there anything I learned from my experience that might help them?"

Letting your pain inspire a heroic quest is one of the surest ways to find fulfillment. Psychologist Scott Allison says, "There's something positive that's happening that you can't see, but will be made clear if you're willing to battle it out."

That's certainly been true for Max Wallack, who created the charity Puzzles to Remember to help people with Alzheimer's disease. Watching his beloved grandmother slip into dementia was one of the toughest things he'd ever been through.

If Max hadn't glimpsed the horror of Alzheimer's up close, he might not have been inspired to help others who were also dealing with it. He transformed his grief into a white-hot determination that inspired him to start his nonprofit, and in 2013, it also drove him to cowrite a kids' book called *Why Did Grandma Put Her Underwear in the Refrigerator?*

As I hope I've made clear, leading a heroic life isn't about developing superhuman strength or pulling off impossible, high-stakes rescues. It simply means being **compassionate and willing to help** in whatever situation we encounter, even if we face risk or discomfort. When we accept this challenge, the difficult things we go through can awaken our determination to make the journey easier for others.

Antoinette Tuff knows that what helped her avert a deadly outcome that August day at McNair was her compassion for someone who was hurting, just as she once had. It's far from easy, but remember: One central goal of the hero's journey is to learn how to cultivate wisdom and empathy in the midst of our greatest struggles. This helps give us the fortitude, skill, and compassion to help others get through theirs.

HEROES FROM HISTORY
Frederick Douglass

Frederick Douglass was born a slave around 1818 in Maryland, and at the time, there was no reason to think he'd ever be free. But despite growing up in captivity, Douglass found ways to expand his mind. Most slaves were not allowed to read or write, but Sophie Auld, his master's wife, taught him in her spare time.

By reading books like *The Columbian Orator*, Douglass educated himself about the debate in the United States over whether to release slaves. **He believed strongly that all slaves deserved to be free,** and he resolved to help them achieve their freedom.

Douglass knew he wouldn't be able to secure freedom for others unless he was free himself, so at age twenty, he left his master's home, donned a sailor's uniform, and boarded a train north, hoping he could evade discovery. As an escaped slave, Douglass did not have the required papers identifying him as a free man, but he satisfied the train conductor by showing him a borrowed seaman's certificate.

After reaching freedom, Douglass continued to develop his skills as a writer and speaker. Over the years, he wrote hundreds of speeches condemning slavery, and his delivery was so moving that he convinced many listeners to rethink their views.

Douglass put himself at great risk by speaking out against slavery. He knew that as an escaped slave, he could be arrested and sent back into captivity. And he knew that even if he succeeded at staying free, he wasn't free from danger. **His speeches incited furor on a regular basis,** and as a result, he faced terrifying ordeals. During one visit to the Midwest, a mob of angry rioters chased him, and later, his house in Rochester, New York, was burned down—likely by arsonists who disliked his abolitionist views.

Douglass struck up a friendship with President Abraham Lincoln during the Civil War, and on January 31, 1865, Douglass's years of dedication to abolishing slavery were rewarded. The Thirteenth Amendment to the United States Constitution—a declaration that slaves were now free—passed through Congress. Nearly 150 years later, on June 19, 2013, a large statue of Douglass debuted at the US Capitol, honoring his heroic commitment to the cause of freedom for all.

9 GROW YOUR TRIBE

In every mythic story, the hero eventually needs help. True lone-wolf heroes are few and far between. Sometimes, this is one of the most important lessons that early obstacles and tests teach the young adventurer: If the hero doesn't get allies or sidekicks, he or she is toast.

The same is true when it comes to heroism in real life. **"It's about getting support where you can,"** says psychologist Robin Rosenberg. "Most superheroes don't operate in isolation. They always have at least one sidekick." So whether you enlist a Robin and an Alfred for your Batman, or you assemble your own real-life Justice League, know that teaming up with others—growing your tribe—is essential, especially if your heroic quest is a longer-term venture.

For instance, consider TJ Berry from Denver, Colorado. In 2013, when he was just seven years old, TJ had an unexpected brush with his own heroic future. He was sitting in the car with his grandmother, and as they idled at a stoplight, TJ spotted a homeless man begging for food just outside his window. "I wanted to help," he remembers, "but the light turned green." As he thought about the starving man, a question burned itself into his brain: *What can I do for all the hungry people out there?*

TJ knew his options were limited—he was too young to do much alone. But he could do something. He wanted to raise money to beat hunger, but as he considered it, he realized it'd be easier if he could convince his friends to help. He asked them, and many said yes. TJ formed an organization called Kids Club so he and his friends could raise money together.

The club's first event was a lemonade and donut stand at TJ's family's garage sale. The sales brought in around three hundred dollars, and Kids Club donated it to the nonprofit organization Hunger Free Colorado, which works to make sure every Coloradan has enough to eat. In the years after that, says TJ's mom, Heather Berry, the club grew to twenty-one members.

Looking back, TJ thinks **reaching out to his friends** was the best decision he could have made—he probably wouldn't have been able to collect half as much money on his own. TJ and his friends got together to talk about the best ways to raise funds, and to date, says Heather, the group has raised more than eleven thousand dollars for a variety of charities.

"We brainstorm ideas," TJ says. "We've gone to the bowling alley and done bowl-a-thons. We've done a dog walk. We've gone to Dart Warz and had Nerf gun battles." The club asked people who attended or took part in these activities to give a modest donation. Club members' parents pitched in from time to time to help plan ways to raise money.

Knowing he can count on his friends' support has supercharged TJ's confidence, and it was a blast to plan events and shoot foam arrows for charity with people he really liked. And as more people learned about Kids Club, the more interest it attracted and the more money it raised. In a way, TJ's original idea became its own community.

THE POWER OF ALLIES

No one thrives alone. We all have family and friends we can enlist as allies in our heroic quest—a group of people who will back our efforts and help bring out the best in us. **Many people experience the power of allies through sports,** particularly team sports like baseball, basketball, or hockey. But we also experience it in individual sports like track. Running a race with friends, with everyone competing and cheering one another, helps everyone run their fastest time.

When it comes to your heroic goal, your mission is to create your own tribe, seeking out helpers who will support your efforts and even inspire you with their own heroic goals.

Of course, sometimes we call people heroes because they stand or act alone when no one else is willing to. But usually, **every hero has supporters** and people who encourage them. Further, we also call people heroes when they inspire others to band together and change the world in ways no one could pull off alone.

There's even a kind of positive peer pressure at work—when we spend time with other people who are dedicated to helping, their enthusiasm spurs us to act. In one study, 76 percent of teens and young people whose friends volunteered said they volunteered, too. Those who said their friends didn't help people, on the other hand, volunteered at far lower rates.

PUTTING YOUR TRIBE TOGETHER

Naturally, you probably already know lots of people who might help you in all sorts of ways. To reap the benefits of teamwork, however, you have to take action to assemble these people into a team. That is, you've got to ask for help and come up with specific requests to fulfill a specific goal. Lots of people *might* help you, but you have to be the one to ask others what you want them to do.

So, first, consider your heroic goal and figure out what jobs need doing and what problems need solving. Then brainstorm: Who among your friends and family could help in those ways? Think as broadly as possible. Seek people of all ages and backgrounds. Some people, like friends, might be important for their enthusiasm, and others, like grandparents, might be able to help by doing things only adults can do.

For instance, when Ethan King built his nonprofit Charity Ball, he connected with dozens of people—kids, teens, and adults—who liked what he was up to and made critical assists when he needed them the most. When Charity Ball was first getting started, Ethan called many friends and family members to ask for donations. Later on, Ethan got an email from a Serbian professional soccer player, Neven Subotić, who had heard about Charity Ball. As the two of them chatted, they forged a strong friendship, and eventually, Subotić helped Ethan design a soccer tournament for Mozambican kids. Ethan appreciates everyone who has contributed to his mission so far. "They're a huge support," Ethan says. "Surrounding yourself with people that care about what you're doing is really important."

To use a team successfully, you have to be a **clear and organized leader.** You have to learn how to call on each person's help and skills at the right times. For example, let's say you'd like to help kids in your school become pen pals with kids from Syria—to learn more about their lives and to show compassion for kids in a war-torn country. But where do you start? First, if you want this to be a school activity, you need the help of a teacher, so talk to teachers first. Then you need someone with connections to a school in Syria. Ask school officials, approach Middle Eastern cultural organizations in the United States, and even search online. **Even ideas that sound simple can involve many steps** and require lots of assistance. Just tackle one at a time, and ask for help as you need it.

Another tried-and-true approach is to gather three or four of your friends and volunteer at the same place, like a local soup kitchen. Chances are, this kind of shared experience will bring you and your friends closer together.

Starting a service or hero club in your school, church, or neighborhood, as TJ did, is also a natural tribe-building strategy. Make sure your club meets in person on a regular basis; this builds camaraderie as you hash out plans and meet challenges. If your school already has a service related club, you might join that or start an offshoot club devoted to a specific cause.

To extend your heroic reach further, use the internet, Facebook, and Twitter to connect with potential tribe members all over the world. If others are pursuing heroic quests similar to yours, you might join forces. As psychologist Dana Klisanin reports, most people feel that they can help others better by using the internet, and taking your heroic quest online—by making a fundraising website, for instance—allows you to deploy an arsenal of superhero qualities, including invisibility, hyper-speed, and the ability to be everywhere at once!

Putting together **a strong tribe is essential** for any heroic quest. As Ethan King says, "I feel like really what society needs is a bunch of kids getting on board,

PROFILES IN COURAGE
Derek & Jessica Simmons

One lazy summer afternoon in 2017 in Panama City, Florida, Derek Simmons and his wife, Jessica, decided to head to the local beach. They looked forward to relaxing as the turquoise waves crashed on the sand.

But it wasn't long before the Simmonses realized something was amiss. Police lights started flashing in the distance, and people on the beach were pointing at a group of swimmers struggling in the water. It looked like they were being pulled out to sea by a rogue rip current.

When Derek and Jessica realized what was going on, they knew they had to do something. *These people are not drowning today,* Jessica thought to herself. *It's not happening. We're going to get them out.*

Derek turned to another man and said, "Let's try to get as many people as we can to form a human chain." A few people doing something positive, and having an effect on the world." As we've seen, you don't need Superman-like abilities to be a hero—you just need the right team, and together you can accomplish many times more than you could alone.

WOW

started to walk toward the water, and Derek kept yelling, **"We need more people!"**

Beachgoers quickly gathered in the water and joined hands, and Derek and Jessica paddled toward the stranded group of swimmers. Once the chain had grown to a few dozen people, Jessica and Derek were able to tow each struggling swimmer back to the end of the chain. The rest of the people in the chain then passed the swimmers safely back to land.

In the end, all of the stranded swimmers were rescued, and none will ever forget Derek and Jessica's selfless act and how they assembled a strong team to carry it out.

"I am so grateful," Roberta Ursrey, one of the rescued swimmers, told a local reporter. "I owe my life and my family's life to them. Without them, we wouldn't be here."

10 TURN HEROIC GOALS INTO A HEROIC LIFE

Paloma Rambana knows what it's like to work twice as hard just to keep up with her class. Paloma has a rare vision problem called Peters anomaly, which means the corneas of her eyes did not develop normally. Most people can easily read large words and signs from two hundred feet away, but Paloma has to stand much closer—about twenty feet away—before the letters finally swim into focus. That can make it hard to read books or see the board at school.

Since she was very young, **Paloma has gotten help** from Florida's state-run Division of Blind Services (DBS). Around the time she started school, the state supplied her with a closed-circuit TV. This TV had a camera and

 magnifying lenses to help her zoom in on words and objects around her classroom, which were then displayed on the device's big screen. But when Paloma was in third grade, the TV broke, and DBS could not afford the three thousand dollars it would cost to buy her a new one.

DBS has helped Paloma as much as it can, but the state doesn't have the resources to help kids like her learn the best they can. "If you're sitting in the back of the classroom and you're six, seven, eight, you're lost," she says. "No matter how hard your teacher tries to help you, you need more help than that."

Today, Paloma's parents pay for a private vision instructor to help her out at school. Paloma is grateful her parents can afford extra services, but she knows a lot of other visually impaired students aren't so lucky. "I found out there are about a thousand kids [like me] in my age group. I realized that if they're not getting funded, **we need to change that.** I thought, 'We can't leave them in the dark, because that's not cool.'"

In 2015, a local nonprofit called the Lighthouse of the Big Bend asked Paloma if she'd work to help students like her get the state funding they needed. She quickly said yes. That year, when she was just nine years old, Paloma lobbied thirteen Florida lawmakers, which meant going into their offices, explaining why visually impaired kids needed more funding, and listening to what the legislators said. "It was nerve-wracking at first," she recalls—especially when her audience turned out to be bigger than she'd predicted. "When I get there and there's like fifty other people with me, I was like, 'Oh, I can't do this.'"

Paloma pushed past her fears and spoke with

lawmakers. The more people she talked to, the more comfortable she felt. Ultimately, her dedication paid off. Later that year, thanks in part to her lobbying efforts, Florida's governor at the time, Rick Scott, approved more than a million dollars in additional state funding for blind and visually impaired kids.

"That was awesome," Paloma says.

But Paloma's heroic journey is far from over. She **achieved her first heroic goal,** but even a million dollars is not enough, and so her next goal is to secure eight million dollars in funding. This is the full amount needed so that kids like her can get maximum classroom support. She knows this is a challenging goal, but she's determined not to give up. "I stay focused—I tell myself, 'I'm going to change the world.' Sometimes the plan doesn't go according to plan, but that's okay."

PLAN FOR SUCCESS, ONE STEP AT A TIME

What heroic goal did you name for yourself in chapter 2? How long do you think it will take to complete? Some goals can be finished in a day, even a moment. When Ethan King gave away his first soccer ball, that selfless gesture took less than ten minutes. But how long does it take to start a nonprofit and give away thousands of soccer balls to needy communities around the world? More than a day, that's for sure.

The truth is, when we set heroic goals for ourselves, we have no idea how long they will take to finish, or what might happen to us or change along the way. Like Ethan's, and like TJ Berry's, our heroic goals may grow to become bigger than we expected. Our lemonade-stand donations may turn into years of charity work. Who knows? The most important thing is to **take the next helpful step that makes sense,** to make plans and set reasonable goals, and to not get too far ahead of ourselves or overwhelmed. We may admire real-life heroes like Frederick Douglass and Malala Yousafzai, who dedicate their lives to heroic causes, but we shouldn't try to compare ourselves to them. Focus on one reasonable goal at a time, and let the rest take care of itself.

Real-life heroes do the same thing. They don't have superpowers; they have determination and stamina. They know that even small actions take planning and that most heroic goals are more of a 5K race than a sprint. Results can take longer to achieve than we expect.

That's why it's important to break big heroic goals into bite-size pieces. If starting a nonprofit organization or raising eight million dollars seems overwhelming, and both are certainly complicated, start by making a list of what you need to do and what sort of help you need. Then map out a schedule and delegate: apply for nonprofit status on Monday, file tax forms on Tuesday, call volunteers on Wednesday, and so on. When she

was working on getting funding for visually-impaired kids, Paloma concentrated on making personal connections, one lawmaker at a time. **"The best goals to set for yourself are attainable goals,"** says psychologist Scott Allison. "Take small steps."

In addition, as you focus on making to-do lists and checking off items, be prepared for your heroic vision to change and evolve. Many of the stories in this book illustrate this. You might be certain, right now, of your goal—to stop bullying, to feed the hungry, to help visually imparied students, to spread the joy of soccer—but this goal may grow, or it might transform into something else as you discover a new problem that needs fixing.

Remember, a heroic goal is defined by the effort to help others. What we do is often less important than that we're doing something.

THE HERO'S JOURNEY BUILDS HEROIC METTLE

In the end, the journey to pursue a heroic goal, whatever it is, is what turns people into real-life heroes. That is the lesson and message of the mythic hero's journey: By working steadily toward a higher purpose, something that makes people's lives better, we mature and become transformed on the inside. Succeed in one heroic goal, and we transform the way we see ourselves. Make everyday acts of selflessness a habit, and we become the kind of real-life heroes others admire, depend on, and seek to emulate.

The hero's journey embodies another truth about heroic goals: By pursing them, we learn lessons we can draw on in all areas of our lives. If we learn to push ourselves to achieve a heroic purpose, that sense of resolve will also benefit us in school, at volunteer jobs, and in relationships.

Not only do we learn important personal skills—like communicating clearly, noticing what others need, and asking for support—but we come to see **heroic opportunities everywhere** we go. That doesn't mean we'll end up working in a so-called "helping profession." It means we become the kind of person who helps others no matter what's going on.

That said, succeeding at heroic goals early in life has a way of influencing career choices. A number of professions are heroic by nature: doctors, nurses, and emergency personnel literally save lives, as do police officers and firefighters. Lawyers speak up for the rights of people who are being treated unfairly; teachers devote themselves to educating and empowering others. There's heroic potential in a wide variety of careers, from journalism to management to computer science. Most of the time, it's just a matter of seeing that potential in whatever path you choose and then realizing it in your own way.

THE FIRST STEP IS THE MOST IMPORTANT ONE

The main thing is, take the first step, regardless of what it is. Choose one heroic goal, even a very simple one, and take concrete action to accomplish it. That's the only way to embark on a hero's journey. Don't simply daydream. Don't be a bystander. Don't see a need and look around waiting for someone else to volunteer. Be the one who does.

Don't worry about what your heroic journey will look like two, ten, or twenty years from today. Simply carry out one selfless action, and then another, and deal with questions and challenges as they arise.

"So many people have good intentions," says Ethan King, the founder of Charity Ball. "They say, 'Oh, that would be nice,' or, 'It would be cool if. . . .' That's where great things start, but too often the thinking process doesn't go beyond that point. **A small act is more powerful than the greatest intention."**

Once you strike out on a heroic path, you discover another secret about living heroically. It provides a certain kind of immortality—but not the fairy-tale kind. It's not like in the classic book *Tuck Everlasting*, about a girl who has a chance to live forever if she drinks water from a magical spring.

You, on the other hand, get to live on in an even more profound way. Your actions to help others will echo and reverberate, improving others' lives in ways you'll never see and that will continue into the future. Mentoring a struggling student may help that person graduate from college, which, in turn, could launch them on a career where they **heal and help** many others. Saving someone from drowning or a heart attack (such as by calling 911) means they will remain alive, which enriches and shapes the lives of everyone they know.

For people like Graceanne Andreessen, Max Wallack, and Paloma Rambana, the promise of that kind of reward motivates them to push through whatever pain, frustration, or obstacles they will inevitably face.

"Your brain doesn't work with negatives," Paloma says. "You need to trust yourself."

We idolize superheroes because they can do what humans can't—passing invisibly through walls, deflecting lightning bolts, leaping tall buildings with a single bound. But as a real-life hero, you get to pull off an even more memorable feat: transforming the world using your very human talents and abilities, and transforming yourself with every good deed.

HEROES FROM HISTORY
Noor Inayat Khan

The descendant of famed Indian ruler Tipu Sultan, Noor Inayat Khan lived a charmed life, growing up in luxury homes all over Europe and studying at fancy schools like the Paris Conservatory. She loved to play the harp and write her own music, and she also wrote children's stories.

Then, in 1939, World War II broke out, and Germany's Nazis took over much of Europe. Khan—then in her midtwenties—escaped from France to Great Britain and decided to devote herself to a heroic cause. She saw German leader Adolf Hitler's dictatorial regime as a threat to the world, and she wanted to help defeat the Nazi aggressors, no matter what.

Khan first volunteered for the British war effort as a member of the Women's Auxiliary Air Force (WAAF) in 1940. But after British officials noticed her fluency in French, they invited her to join the elite ranks of the Special Operations

Executive, the renowned British spy corps. She accepted in 1943 and moved to Paris, France's Nazi-occupied capital. Her perfect French made her an asset as she operated the wireless radios that allowed the British to talk with allies in the French Resistance movement. Thanks to Khan's efforts, Allied forces were able to coordinate secret operations in France and deliver weapons where they were most needed.

In October of 1943, Khan's daring mission was cut short when German policemen stormed into a Paris apartment where she was staying and arrested her. The Germans tortured her to try to get information about British spy operations, but she refused to tell her captors what she'd been up to. In September 1944, Nazi soldiers shot her at the Dachau concentration camp, and she died shouting, "Liberty!"

QUESTIONS FOR DISCUSSION

Chapter 1 introduces a variety of definitions of heroism.

In particular, it notes that being heroic doesn't necessarily mean putting yourself at physical risk. What does being a hero mean to you? What are some actions people take that qualify as "heroic"?

Chapter 2 asks you to identify a heroic goal or mission that truly inspires you.

What problems in the world today require heroic action? Can you identify some of the ways people are already trying to solve these problems? Do these examples provide models for an action you could take?

Chapter 3 describes the universal mythic story of the hero's journey, in which a hero devotes him- or herself to an important goal, overcomes trials, and ultimately succeeds.

What stories have you read or seen that embody the hero's journey? In what ways can these stories inspire us as we pursue our own heroic goals?

Chapter 4 discusses how role models and mentors can help us as we pursue a heroic path.

What are some important qualities a role model or mentor should have? Who are some of your role models? What do you respect and admire about them?

In Chapter 5, Dave Rendall advises people to embrace their inner freak.

What does being willing to stand out have to do with taking a heroic approach to life?

Chapter 6 describes how some schools are experimenting with different methods of heroic education.

Do you think heroic qualities can be taught? If so, which ones, and what are some ways to teach them? If not, why not?

Chapter 7 discusses how to evaluate and minimize the risks of heroic actions.

Is it important to keep yourself safe while helping others? What risks would you take in different situations, depending on what's at stake? How would you protect yourself from unnecessary harm?

Chapter 8 talks about how helping others sometimes forces us to face our own pain and hard times.

Then again, sometimes our struggles are what inspire us to help people facing similar problems. What are some tough or difficult situations you've been through? What advice would you give to people going through the same thing? How might sharing difficult experiences help people?

Chapter 9 discusses the importance of allies and the power of group efforts.
What are some situations where working as a group would make more sense than working alone? On the other hand, when might it be important to stand apart from the crowd?

Chapter 10 advises breaking large heroic goals into small, doable steps.
This helps us avoid burnout and feeling overwhelmed. Do you ever get overwhelmed by big goals or problems? What are some ways you avoid this or recapture your zest and enthusiasm?

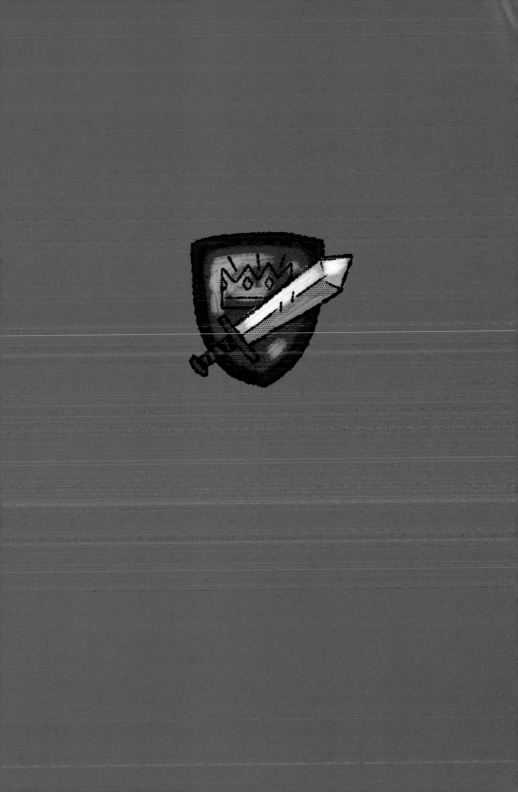

SOURCES

The stories and quotes in this book come from a variety of sources. Many real-life heroes and experts were interviewed by the author for this book, and these are listed separately. Additional published sources and further resources are listed by chapter.

PERSONAL INTERVIEWS

Scott Allison, conversation with author, February 18, 2016.

Graceanne Andreessen, conversations with author, July 21, 2013, and September 8, 2017.

TJ Berry, conversation with author, March 24, 2016.

Juliana Davis, email correspondence with author, May 24, 2016.

Megan Felt, email correspondence and conversation with author, September 30, 2014, and September 21, 2017.

Leanne Joyce, conversation with author, August 1, 2017.

Ethan King, conversation with author, March 4, 2016.

Dominique Moceanu, conversation with author, March 7, 2017.

David Nance, conversation with author, April 27, 2016.

Stephen Post, conversation with author, April 20, 2016.

Paloma Rambana, conversation with author, May 18, 2016.

David Rendall, conversation with author, February 23, 2016.

Robin Rosenberg, conversation with author, April 15, 2016.

Marcos Ugarte, conversation with author, May 10, 2013.

Max Wallack, conversation with author, May 16, 2013.

Philip Zimbardo, conversations and email correspondence with author, multiple occasions from 2010 through 2013.

INTRODUCTION

Masterson, Teresa, "Teen Grabs Wheel, Saves School Bus as Driver Has Heart Attack," NBC 10, January 26, 2012, http://www .nbcphiladelphia.com/news/local/Teen-Grabs-Wheel-as -School-Bus-Driver-Has-Heart-Attack-138075358.html.

O'Rourke, John, "A 16-Year-Old Takes On a Disease of the Elderly," BU Today, April 30, 2013, http://www.bu.edu/today/2013/a-16 -year-old-takes-on-a-disease-of-the-elderly.

Svoboda, Elizabeth, "Could You Be a Hero?" Scholastic Choices, November/ December 2013.

Svoboda, Elizabeth, What Makes a Hero?: The Surprising Science of Selflessness (New York: Penguin Current, 2013).

Wallack, Max, "The Responsibility of Max: The Incredible Story of Puzzles to Remember," My Name My Story, http:// mynamemystory.org/max-wallack.html.

For more information:

The Heroic Imagination Project, heroicimagination.org

Puzzles to Remember, www.puzzlestoremember.org

CHAPTER 1

Abbey, Jennifer, "Oregon Teen Rescues 7-Year-Old Neighbor From House Fire," ABC News, September 25, 2012, http://abcnews .go.com/US/oregon-teen-rescues-year-neighbor-house-fire /story?Id=17320734.

Aristotle, Nichomachean Ethics, trans. D. P. Chase (New York: Cosimo Classics, 2007).

Berger, Susan, "Bennet Omalu, Doctor Who Raised Alarm Bells about NFL Head Injuries, on Racism in U.S. Science," Washington Post, December 29, 2015, https://www.washingtonpost.com /news/to-your-health/wp/2015/12/29/bennet-omalu-doctor -who-raised-alarm-bells-about-nfl-head-injuries-on-racism -in-u-s-science.

Brickman, Philip, Dan Coates, and Ronnie Janoff-Bulman, "Lottery Winners and Accident Victims: Is Happiness Relative?" *Journal of Personality and Social Psychology* 36, no. 8 (1978): 917–27.

Dodd, Johnny, "'Miracle on the Hudson' Pilot Chesley 'Sully' Sullenberger Says Post-Flight Fame Was 'Challenging, Intense,'" *People*, September 7, 2016, http://people.com/movies /chesley-sully-sullenberger-miracle-on-the-hudson-pilot-talks -post-flight-fame.

Giraffe Heroes Project, "History of the Giraffe Heroes Project," https://www.giraffe.org/about-us/history-of-the-giraffe -heroes-project.

Itkowitz, Colby, "For 79 Years, This Groundbreaking Harvard Study Has Searched for the Key to Happiness. Should It Keep Going?" *Washington Post*, April 17, 2017, https://www.washingtonpost .com/news/inspired-life/wp/2017/04/17/this-harvard-study -found-the-one-thing-we-need-for-happier-healthier-lives-but -researchers-say-theres-more-to-learn.

Library of Congress, "Meet Amazing Americans: Harriet Tubman," *America's Story*, http://www.americaslibrary.gov/aa/tubman /aa_tubman_rail_1.html.

McFadden, Robert D., "Pilot Is Hailed After Jetliner's Icy Plunge," *New York Times*, January 15, 2009, http://www.nytimes.com /2009/01/16/nyregion/16crash.html.

MSNBC.com staff, "N.Y. Jet Crash Called 'Miracle on the Hudson,'" *NBC News*, January 15, 2009, http://www.nbcnews.com /id/28678669/ns/us_news-life/t/ny-jet-crash-called-miracle -hudson/#.Wax9xDOZOqA.

Pletcher, Kenneth, "Indian History: Salt March," *Britannica.com*, March 4, 2010.

Post, Stephen G., "It's Good to be Good: Science Says It's So," *Health Progress*, July-August 2009.

Shenker, Israel, "Golda Meir: Peace and Arab Acceptance Were Goals of Her 5 Years as Premier," *New York Times*, December 9,

1978, http://www.nytimes.com/learning/general/onthisday
/bday/0503.html?mcubz=1.

Shiner, Linda, "Sully's Tale," *Air & Space Magazine*, February 18, 2009.

Tretkoff, Ernie, "This Month in Physics History, March 16, 1938:
Katharine Blodgett Patents Anti-reflective Coatings," *APS News*,
March 2007, https://www.aps.org/publications/apsnews/200703
/history.cfm.

Zeno Franco, Kathy Blau, and Philip Zimbardo, "Heroism: A
Conceptual Analysis and Differentiation Between Heroic Action
and Altruism," *Review of General Psychology* 15, no. 2 (2011): 99–113.

For more information:

Christoph von Toggenburg's website, https://www.vontoggenburg.com

Giraffe Heroes Project, www.giraffe.org

Real Life Super Hero Project, http://reallifesuperheroes.com

CHAPTER 2

Abaurrea, Nate, "SoccerNation Sitdown: Ethan King and Charity
Ball," *SoccerNation*, July 14, 2017, https://www.soccernation
.com/soccernation-sitdown-ethan-king-and-charity-ball.

Cotliar, Sharon, "Teen Gives 4,000 Soccer Balls to Kids Around the
World Who Can't Afford Them," *People*, March 13, 2014, http://
people.com/human-interest/teen-gives-4000-soccer-balls-to
-kids-around-the-world-who-cant-afford-them.

Medoff, Rafael, "The Holocaust Messenger Who Confronted FDR,"
Jewish News Service, July 15, 2013.

Shute, Lauren, "Teenager Ethan King Changes Lives, One Soccer
Ball at a Time," *Sports Illustrated Kids*, June 30, 2014, https://
www.sikids.com/si-kids/2016/01/12/changing-lives-one
-soccer-ball-time.

Yad Vashem: The World Holocaust Remembrance Center, "The
Righteous Among the Nations: Jan Karski," http://www
.yadvashem.org/righteous/stories/karski.

For more information:

Charity Ball, https://charityball.org

Positive Impact for Kids, https://positiveimpactforkids.org

CHAPTER 3

Brooks, Edward, *Story of the Iliad* (Philadelphia: Penn Publishing Company, 1902).

Campbell, Joseph, *The Hero With A Thousand Faces* (Princeton, NJ: Princeton University Press, 2004).

"Malala Yousafzai—Facts," Nobelprize.org, Nobel Media AB 2014, September 12, 2017, https://www.nobelprize.org/nobel_prizes /peace/laureates/2014/yousafzai-facts.html.

Stephens, Greg J., et al. "Speaker–Listener Neural Coupling Underlies Successful Communication," *Proceedings of the National Academy of Sciences* 27, no. 32 (August 10, 2010): 14425–30.

Walsh, Declan, "Taliban Gun Down Girl Who Spoke Up For Rights," *New York Times*, October 9, 2012, http://www.nytimes.com /2012/10/10/world/asia/teen-school-activist-malala-yousafzai -survives-hit-by-pakistani-taliban.html?mcubz=1.

Yousafzai, Malala, "The Full Text: Malala Yousafzai Delivers Defiant Riposte to Taliban Militants with Speech to the UN General Assembly," *The Independent*, July 12, 2013, http://www .independent.co.uk/news/world/asia/the-full-text-malala -yousafzai-delivers-defiant-riposte-to-taliban-militants-with -speech-to-the-un-8706606.html.

CHAPTER 4

Hurd, N. M., et al., "Negative adult influences and the protective effects of role models: A study with urban adolescents," *Journal of Youth and Adolescence* 38, no. 38 (July 2009): 777–89.

Mayer, Jack, *Life in a Jar: The Irena Sendler Project* (Middlebury, VT: Long Trail Press, 2011).

Yousafzai, Ziauddin, "My Daughter, Malala," *TED*, March 2014, https://www.ted.com/talks/ziauddin_yousafzai_my_daughter _malala/transcript?language=en.

Toner, Kathleen, "Meet the Superman Saving the Sun Bears of Malaysia," *CNN*, July 27, 2017, http://www.cnn.com /2017/07/27/world/cnn-hero-siew-te-wong-bornean-sun -bear-conservation-centre.

For more information:

Bornean Sun Bear Conservation Centre, www.bsbcc.org.my

CNN Heroes, www.cnn.com/specials/cnn-heroes

Life in a Jar: The Irena Sendler Project, irenasendler.org

Lowell Milken Center for Unsung Heroes, lowellmilkencenter.org

CHAPTER 5

Hornsey, Matthew J., et al. "On Being Loud and Proud: Non-Conformity and Counter-Conformity to Group Norms," *British Journal of Social Psychology* 42, no. 3 (September 2003): 319–35.

For more information:

David Rendall's website, www.drendall.com

CHAPTER 6

Condon, Paul, et al., "Meditation Increases Compassionate Responses to Suffering," *Psychological Science* 24, no. 10 (August 21, 2013): 2125–27, http://journals.sagepub.com /doi/abs/10.1177/0956797613485603.

Dweck, Carol, *Mindset: The New Psychology of Success* (New York: Random House, 2006).

The Heroic Imagination Project, "The Bystander Effect: Transforming Bystanders Into Heroic Actors," lesson plan shared with author, January 14, 2014.

The Heroic Imagination Project, "Testimonials."

Peace in Schools, "Mindfulness Research," https://www
.peaceinschools.org/mindfulness-research.

Peace in Schools, "Teen Voices," https://www.peaceinschools.org
/what-teens-say.

Peace in Schools, Wilson High School, Portland, Oregon, class
observed by author, May 6, 2015.

Zimbardo, Philip, "The Stanford Prison Experiment: A Simulation
Study on the Psychology of Imprisonment," Stanford Prison
Experiment website, http://www.prisonexp.org.

For more information:

Peace in Schools, www.peaceinschools.org

CHAPTER 7

Acosta, Roberto, "Explicit 'After School' App Should Be Removed
From Apple Store, Say Swartz Creek Student's Petitions," mlive
.com, December 3, 2014.

Davis, Juliana, and Elizabeth Long, "Help Stop Anonymous Apps
Like Yik-Yak, After School, and Slam High By Changing Apple
and Google's App Rules," Change.org petition, 2014, https://
www.change.org/p/google-inc-help-stop-anonymous-apps
-like-yik-yak-after-school-and-slam-high-by-changing-apple
-and-google-s-app-rules.

Deterline, Brooke, "How to Cultivate Ethical Courage," *Greater Good
Magazine*, June 2, 2016, https://greatergood.berkeley.edu/article
/item/how_to_cultivate_ethical_courage.

DiManno, Rosie, "Newmarket Teen Reaches Out to Save Suicidal
Boy After Seeing Tumblr Postings," *Toronto Star*, March 3, 2012,
https://www.thestar.com/news/crime/2012/03/03/newmarket
_teen_reaches_out_to_save_suicidal_boy_after_seeing
_tumblr_postings.html.

Henderson, Lynne, Menlo College (Menlo Park, CA), author

observation of students practicing "courageous conversations," November 1, 2011.

Hoose, Philip, *It's Our World, Too!: Young People Who Are Making a Difference* (New York: Farrar, Straus, & Giroux, 2002).

Zimbardo, Philip, "Heroism and the Heroic Imagination Project," *PsychologyToday.com*, August 25, 2017, https://www.psychologytoday.com/blog/the-time-cure/201708/heroism-and-the-heroic-imagination-project.

For more information:
Courageous Leadership, www.thecourage2lead.com

CHAPTER 8

"911 Call Captures School Employee Talking Down Gunman," *NPR*, August 22, 2013, http://www.npr.org/2013/08/22/214576953/911-call-captures-school-employee-talking-down-gunman.

"Frederick Douglass: Journalist, Civil Rights Activist, Author, Government Official," Biography.com, https://www.biography.com/people/frederick-douglass-9278324.

Library of Congress, "Frederick Douglass Timeline," Frederick Douglass Papers at the Library of Congress, https://www.loc.gov/collections/frederick-douglass-papers/articles-and-essays/frederick-douglass-timeline/1818-to-1835

Murphy, Justin, "Rochester Library Renamed for Frederick Douglass," *Democrat & Chronicle*, March 21, 2016, http://www.democratandchronicle.com/story/news/2016/03/21/highland-library-frederick-douglass/81980518.

Pershing, Ben, "Frederick Douglass Statue Unveiled in the Capitol," *Washington Post*, June 19, 2013, https://www.washingtonpost.com/local/dc-politics/frederick-douglass-statue-unveiled-in-the-capitol/2013/06/19/a64916cc-d906-11e2-a9f2-42ee3912ae0e_story.html?utm_term=.b6933af035fb.

Staub, Ervin, and Johanna Vollhardt, "Inclusive Altruism Born of

Suffering: The Relationship Between Adversity and Prosocial Attitudes and Behavior Toward Disadvantaged Outgroups," *American Journal of Orthopsychiatry* 81, no. 3 (July 2011): 307–15.

Tuff, Antoinette, *Prepared for a Purpose* (Bloomington, MN: Bethany House, 2014).

CHAPTER 9

Dion, Eryn, "Amazing Human Chain Formed to Rescue Drowning Family in PCB," *Panama City News Herald*, July 10, 2017, http://www.nwfdailynews.com/news/20170710/amazing-human-chain-formed-to-rescue-drowning-family-in-pcb.

"The DoSomething.org Index on Young People and Volunteering," DoSomething.org, 2012, https://www.dosomething.org/sites/default/files/blog/2012-Web-Singleview_0.pdf.

Klisanin, Dana, "Introducing the Cyberhero Archetype: Research Identifies a New Form of Networked Heroism," *Psychology Today*, July 6, 2012, https://www.psychologytoday.com/blog/digital-altruism/201207/introducing-the-cyberhero-archetype.

Luscombe, Richard, "At Least 80 People Form Human Chain to Rescue Stranded Group in Gulf of Mexico," *The Guardian*, July 11, 2017, https://www.theguardian.com/us-news/2017/jul/11/80-people-form-human-chain-rescue-gulf-of-mexico-florida.

Mettler, Katie, "Rip Currents Swept Away a Florida Family. Then Beachgoers Formed a Human Chain," *Washington Post*, July 11, 2017, https://www.washingtonpost.com/news/morning-mix/wp/2017/07/11/a-riptide-swept-away-a-florida-family-then-beachgoers-formed-a-human-chain/?utm_term=.6bb3c295bfbd.

Shute, Lauren, "Teenager Ethan King Changes Lives, One Soccer Ball at a Time," *Sports Illustrated Kids*, June 30, 2014, https://www.sikids.com/si-kids/2016/01/12/changing-lives-one-soccer-ball-time.

CHAPTER 10

Basu, Shrabani, *Spy Princess* (Stroud, UK: Sutton, 2009).

"CCTVs/ Video Magnifiers," American Foundation for the Blind, http://www.afb.org/prodBrowseCatResults.aspx?CatID=53.

Keating, Susan, "10-Year-Old Blind Florida Girl Raises Over $1 Million to Help Other Kids Like Her: 'Be Brave, the Result Is Worth It,'" *People*, May 30, 2016, http://people.com/human -interest/paloma-rambana-blind-florida-girl-raises-over-1 -million-to-help-others.

Tonkin, Boyd, "Noor Anayat Khan: The princess who became a spy," *The Independent*, February 20, 2006, http://www.independent .co.uk/arts-entertainment/books/features/noor-anayat-khan -the-princess-who-became-a-spy-6108704.html.

For more information:

Paloma's Dream, www.palomasdream.org

Noor Inayat Khan Memorial Trust, www.noormemorial.org

ABOUT THE AUTHOR

Elizabeth Svoboda is a writer in San Jose, California, and the author of *What Makes a Hero?: The Surprising Science of Selflessness*. She loves telling the stories of everyday heroes who are all around us. When not writing, she enjoys painting, volunteering, and chasing after her two young sons, Nate and Theo.

ABOUT THE ILLUSTRATOR

Chris Hajny is an illustrator and product designer based in Minneapolis, Minnesota. He's co-founder of collaborative arts space Light Grey Art Lab, and he spends most of his free time playing board games and petting all the animals that will let him.